Lecture Notes
in Business Information Processing   **488**

Series Editors

Wil van der Aalst, *RWTH Aachen University, Aachen, Germany*

Sudha Ram, *University of Arizona, Tucson, AZ, USA*

Michael Rosemann, *Queensland University of Technology, Brisbane, QLD, Australia*

Clemens Szyperski, *Microsoft Research, Redmond, WA, USA*

Giancarlo Guizzardi, *University of Twente, Enschede, The Netherlands*

LNBIP reports state-of-the-art results in areas related to business information systems and industrial application software development – timely, at a high level, and in both printed and electronic form.

The type of material published includes

- Proceedings (published in time for the respective event)
- Postproceedings (consisting of thoroughly revised and/or extended final papers)
- Other edited monographs (such as, for example, project reports or invited volumes)
- Tutorials (coherently integrated collections of lectures given at advanced courses, seminars, schools, etc.)
- Award-winning or exceptional theses

LNBIP is abstracted/indexed in DBLP, EI and Scopus. LNBIP volumes are also submitted for the inclusion in ISI Proceedings.

Eduard Babkin · Joseph Barjis ·
Pavel Malyzhenkov · Vojtěch Merunka ·
Martin Molhanec
Editors

Model-Driven Organizational and Business Agility

Third International Workshop, MOBA 2023
Zaragoza, Spain, June 12–13, 2023
Revised Selected Papers

 Springer

Editors
Eduard Babkin [ID]
HSE University
Nizhny Novgorod, Russia

Joseph Barjis
San Jose State University
San Jose, CA, USA

Pavel Malyzhenkov [ID]
HSE University
Nizhny Novgorod, Russia

Vojtěch Merunka [ID]
Czech Technical University in Prague
Prague, Czech Republic

Martin Molhanec [ID]
Czech Technical University in Prague
Prague, Czech Republic

ISSN 1865-1348   ISSN 1865-1356 (electronic)
Lecture Notes in Business Information Processing
ISBN 978-3-031-45009-9   ISBN 978-3-031-45010-5 (eBook)
https://doi.org/10.1007/978-3-031-45010-5

This Springer imprint is published by the registered company Springer Nature Switzerland AG
The registered company address is: Gewerbestrasse 11, 6330 Cham, Switzerland

Paper in this product is recyclable.

Preface

The current reality in the corporate world demands enterprises to be agile in every aspect. This implies agility as an organization, agility in responding to changes, and agility in strategy and execution. All this culminates in agility in delivering products (solutions) to the customer. This latter has fostered the development of various agile frameworks and agile development approaches. However, the agile practice is often driven by mere pragmatics and relevance, that is, applying agile with little research and, often, little rigour. This presents opportunities for researchers to look at the agile field through the lens of research and bring more rigour to it.

Software engineering or any system development has essential intersections with business engineering, management consulting, customer engagement, and many more. This makes modern software or any system development a cross-functional activity. This recognition brings software engineering beyond merely writing program code. Agile practice emphasizes that requirements emerge as the software system goes through the development process. Agile practice does not even assume that the requirements must be completely and accurately identified at the beginning of the development life cycle but rather continuously explored.

The international workshop on Model-driven Organizational and Business Agility (MOBA) was launched to encourage scientific inquiries into agile practice and agility in a wider context. In this wider context, this means an entire enterprise. The role of models and modelling was especially taken into focus. As a community, MOBA aims to become an incubator and platform for original and innovative ideas that are in their infancy and need expert discussion, insights, and criticism from peers. In this sense, MOBA facilitates junior researchers' participation and success.

The central tenet of an agile mindset is to develop a capability to respond rapidly to changes, reduce uncertainty by iteratively exploring the solution context and scope, and incrementally deliver values to the customers. In this sense, agile practice has equal merit in developing an IT application, i.e., software engineering, or non-IT specialisms such as marketing, operations, human resources, legal, etc. However, in its current state, agile practice is dominantly applied in the IT domain as it is applied in all stages of the life cycle of modern IT systems. This way, only a fraction of the true potential that agile practice can bring to enterprises is utilized. So, the vast unexplored opportunities and the corresponding changelessness of agile practice need scientific inquiry, research, and rigorous solutions.

To explore these opportunities and address the potential challenges, the MOBA Workshop aims to explore organizational and business agility or Enterprise Agility scientifically and pragmatically. In 2023 eighteen submissions were made to the workshop. After double-blind reviews the program committee accepted nine of them. All accepted papers had at least two reviewers. MOBA tries to find analogies and the common theoretical background for model-driven studies of organizational and business agility from various perspectives ranging from formal mathematical approaches to soft skills by which it tries to harmonize them.

To model and study organizational and business agility from a system perspective, we inevitably should combine best practices from industry, enterprise architecture, semantic interoperability, model-driven design of information systems, model validation, and business value co-creation.

Recognizing strong relations between Digital Twin and Agile development, the MOBA workshop expressed an interest in more profound understanding and modelling of new organisational and business agility phenomena when an organisation incorporates Digital Twin solutions into its structure. Several contributions this year lay foundations for research in this area, and we expect to see more valuable contributions in the next year.

June 2023

Eduard Babkin
Joseph Barjis
Pavel Malyzhenkov
Vojtěch Merunka
Martin Molhanec

Organization

MOBA 2023 was organized in cooperation with CAISE 2023 (Zaragoza, Spain)

Executive Committee

General Chair

Eduard Babkin   HSE University, Russia

Program Chairs

Joseph Barjis	San José State University, USA
Pavel Malyzhenkov	HSE University, Russia
Vojtech Merunka	Czech Technical University in Prague, Czech Republic
Martin Molhanec	Czech Technical University in Prague, Czech Republic

Program Committee

Eduard Babkin	HSE University, Russia
Joseph Barjis	San José State University, USA
Anna Bobkowska	Gdansk University of Technology, Poland
Alexander Bock	University of Duisburg-Essen, Germany
Mahmoud Boufaida	Mentouri University of Constantine, Algeria
Simona Colucci	Politecnico di Bari, Italy
Francesco M. Donini	Università della Tuscia, Italy
Sergio Guerreiro	Instituto Superior Tecnico, University of Lisbon, Portugal
Giancarlo Guizzardi	Free University of Bozen-Bolzano, Italy
Georg Grossmann	UniSA STEM, Australia
Kristina Hettne	Leiden University, The Netherlands
Frantisek Hunka	University of Ostrava, Czech Republic
Dmitry Kudryavtsev	Digital City Planner Oy, Finland
Russell Lock	Loughborough University, UK
Pavel Malyzhenkov	HSE University, Russia

Contents

Strategic Agility in Practice: Experts' Opinions on the Applicability of a Model-Driven Framework

Konstantinos Tsilionis[iD], Yves Wautelet[✉][iD], Lena Truyers, and Yan Din

KU Leuven, Leuven, Belgium
{konstantinos.tsilionis,yves.wautelet,lena.truyers,
yan.din}@kuleuven.be

Abstract. Strategic agility constitutes a topic that is more and more popular in the field of IT adoption. Traditional (operational) agile development has indeed been very successful and has profoundly impacted the industry of software development so that professionals are aiming to apply the receipt at an higher level. Strategic agility is nevertheless mostly considered as something that can be obtained through the right mentality and organizational structures rather than a method that can be applied in a way. Strategic Agile Model Driven IT Governance (StratAMoDrIGo) framework has proposed a model-driven methodology to be applied in an organization to help it dealing with moving business context, recognize strategic opportunities and adopt them in an agile way. The framework has been presented and validated in a journal article, the present paper further collects opinions and considerations of industry experts on strategic agility in general and on StrataMoDrIGo in particular.

Keywords: Strategic Agility · Model-driven IT Governance · Agile · StrataMoDrIGo

1 Introduction

The notion of strategic agility can be explained as an organization's capacity to fully enable three main types of dynamic capabilities, i.e., the capacity to sense and shape opportunities (sensing), the capacity to seize opportunities (seizing), and the capacity to maintain competitiveness through reconfiguring the enterprise's assets (shifting) [10]. The latter is to be considered as inherently paradoxical [6, 14, 17]. Indeed, on the one hand, it dictates organizations to develop (and commit to) a comprehensive and well-articulated strategy that sets them apart from the competition; and, on the other hand, organizations are required to allow for a certain level of flexibility to (i) accommodate the flow of new ideas, (ii) incorporate new technologies, and (iii) be able to maneuver efficiently in the face of external (or internal) changes in the business context. Consequently, there seems to be a need for comprehensive frameworks, clear processes, or any kind of exhaustive method that would make organizations refrain from having to rely on unintegrated (ad-hoc) processes in their effort to reach a state of strategic agility.

In this setting, Tsilionis & Wautelet [23] propose the Strategic Agile Model Driven IT Governance (StratAMoDrIGo) framework, a conceptual modeling-driven approach

© The Author(s), under exclusive license to Springer Nature Switzerland AG 2023
E. Babkin et al. (Eds.): MOBA 2023, LNBIP 488, pp. 1–15, 2023.
https://doi.org/10.1007/978-3-031-45010-5_1

aimed at supporting organizations to achieve a state of strategic agility. StratAMoD-rIGo further enhances the Model Driven IT Governance (MoDrIGo) framework [26] – which is a more classical IT governance framework – with fast decision mechanisms at strategic level to quickly take advantage of strategic opportunities. The latter are technologies having a structural impact on the organization's finances or the way it conducts its business. The impact brought by these strategic opportunities in terms of strategic, stakeholder and user value is studied by the application of the framework. The inclusion of StratAMoDrIGo in the organization's practices is intended to enhance (i) its sensing capability by creating an opportunity-aware culture, (ii) its seizing capability by offering a concrete way to evaluate the organizational impact of opportunities' adoption, and (iii) its shifting capability by highlighting how organizational resources and structures can be reconfigured for the adoption of the opportunities. Overall, the key idea of StratAMoDrIGo is purposed to offer a practical roadmap on how diverse organizations can achieve a state of strategic agility. The model-driven approach emphasizes primarily on the interdependence that has to be sustained between any top-down delineation of strategic objectives and the changes that occur externally (and/or internally) at the level of the organization. Simultaneously, StratAMoDrIGo aspires to promulgate the intentions of any stakeholder having an implicit interest in the adaptation of strategic opportunities; the latter could be schematically described as any novel technology intended to augment (i) employee productivity, (ii) customer satisfaction, (iii) competitive advantage, and (iv) overall capital gains, for the entirety of any organization. StratAMoDrIGo aims to counteract the command-and-control design of various frameworks including aspects of strategic agility (e.g., SAFe 5.1 [16]); such designs mostly favor the top-down indoctrination of a series of complicated operationalization procedures that end-up impeding the bottom-up dissemination of agile core principles.

The present paper can be construed as a more empiricist approach towards the strategic agility research strand. More specifically, we offer the stand to professionals (experts) implicated in strategic agility implementation projects within contemporary organizations. The main Research Question this paper aims to answer is: *What is the perception of industry experts on strategic agility and a framework for implemening it in a model-driven way (i.e. StratAMoDrIGo)?* We indeed want to understand how these experts perceive the notion of strategic agility and how they implement it into the matrices of their organizational structures. Most importantly, we present these experts with the structure and internal workings of StratAMoDrIGo to receive some lessons about the latter's applicability and ease of use into the setting of a modern-day enterprise.

2 Background: The StrataMoDrIGo Framework

Figure 1 depicts StrataMoDrIGo's reference ontology documenting the key concepts for dealing with strategic agility in an organizational setting. In short, the *Business_Context* represents the environment the organization is dealing with. As example of an instance could be the Covid-19 pandemic or other game changing events like a merger, new trends in customer habits, new behavior in employees' work, etc. [23]. The core strategy may be impacted by the business context (see *drives* relationship) between the *Business_Context* and the *Strategic_Objective* class. A changing *Busi-*

ness_Context can drive one or more *Strategic_Opportunities* represented by the *Strategic_Opportunity* class. The adoption of the *Strategic_Opportunity* can thus sustain preexisting *Strategic_Objectives* and/or new ones driven by the *Business_Context*. When a *Strategic_Opportunity* sustains a *Strategic_Objective* it delivers *Strategic_Value* to the organization. More information notably on the management-level can be found in [23].

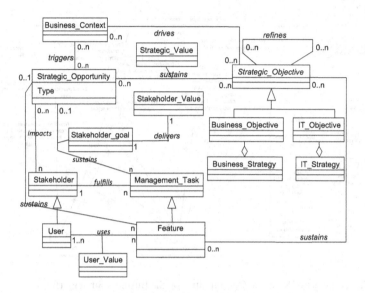

Fig. 1. StrataMoDriGo's Ontology (from [23]).

Figure 2 gives an instance of the strategic-level where a positive contribution from the *Strategic Opportunity* to *Strategic Objectives* can be seen; this represents *Strategic Value*. The instance of the corresponding managerial level in the form of a Strategic Rationale Diagram [30] can be found in [23]. Further, the operational implementation can be realized using a traditional agile method; the rationale tree [27] is then used to conceptually link both levels. The meta-model and these representations have been presented to experts to further collect opinions (see Sect. 3.3).

3 Research Approach, Data Sampling Technique and Data Collection

3.1 Research Approach

There is a plethora of academic studies addressing the topic of strategic agility from a strategic management or human resources' perspective (see [1,6,7,17]) but these do not really provide any practical guidance on how to reach a higher level of strategic agility. Also, to the best of our knowledge, there is a lack of studies that perform empirical

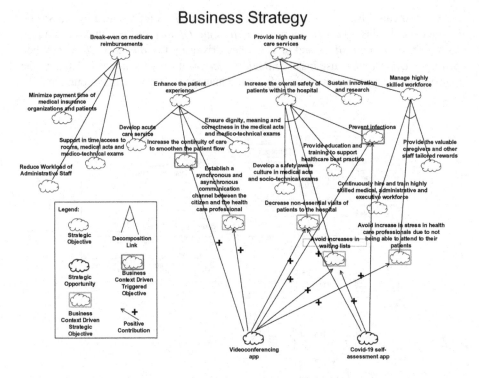

Fig. 2. Impact of Strategic Opportunities on the Business Strategy (from [23]).

observations on the actual activators or inhibitors of strategic agility within the complex and ever-changing structure of modern-day enterprises. We thus start with performing an exploratory study [3,4,20] targeted at gathering, investigating, comprehending, and performing in-between comparisons of various strategic agility definitions attributed to a specific pool of experts. We chose to be truly exploratory and rely on the collection of empirical data to identify, gather, and iteratively refine some of the strategic agility characteristics that seem to predominate in the perception of professionals; their competences were then used to perform a practical evaluation of StratAMoDrIGo.

An abductive research approach [20] (i.e., a combination of deduction and induction) was adopted due to the iterative exploration of the inference that best explains empirical data [21]. Indeed, the setting of our research began with the identification of key strategic-agility project coordinators within several technology-oriented organizations and the collection of data exploring these organizations' in-situ (or planned) strategic agility capabilities. We wanted to capture rich in-content through these professionals' opinions, experiences and expertise so that a qualitative research methodology [15,19] was adopted via the conduct of semi-structured interviews.

As a mean to the end of studying strategic agility's perception and the StrataMoD-RIGo framework, we had to create an appropriate interview protocol. The creation of the latter had to be dealt in a way rendering it capable of (i) collecting data for the factual exploration encompassing the nature of strategic agility, and (ii) properly exposing StratAMoDrIGo to the acuity of these experts so they can consider its potentiality as a strategic agility facilitator. Our iterative process for the creation of the interview protocol followed the logic of the 'Interview Protocol Refinement Framework' described in the study of Castillo-Montoya [5]. Practically, this means that we did not use the same set of questions for all the interviewees; rather, following the premise of Evers & Wu [9] and Yin [29], we treated each instance of our sample as a transmitter of a cohesive amount of empirical knowledge capable of releasing information that can be used for the reevaluation, readjustment, and evolution of the interview protocol.

3.2 Data Sampling Technique and Data Collection

The nature of our research dictated the use of a purposive sampling technique [8] in order to determine a pool of respondents that possess a specific set of traits. To be specific, our target sample should primarily consist of individuals that are academically trained and professionally competent in functions related to business information management, business and IT alignment, and/or software development. These individuals should have a broad (technical or managerial) view on subjects related to the implementation of agile frameworks and methodologies; executives and/or consultants that would be well-versed in matters closely associated to the optimization of business and IT processes could be particularly suitable in terms of providing subjective definitions for the notion of strategic agility. There was no limitation in terms to the specifics of an expert's industry since we were aiming to capture multiple viewpoints from people in different sectors. An initial number of candidates was selected primarily from the professional network (using LinkedIn) of one of the members of the research team with the consent of the remaining members. A snowball sampling technique [20] was then followed from those initial cases in order to retrieve additional survey candidates whose profiles could adhere to the selection criteria as set by the research team. At the end, a total number of 13 candidates expressed interest in participating in the survey but 5 were eliminated from the process as their roles were related to the formulation of business strategies and not so much involved with the implementation of agile solutions; this brought the final number of participants to 8 which was close to what Hennink & Kaiser [13] and Guest et al. [11] describe as the point of data saturation (the former estimate it to be reached in between 9 and 17 interview cases and the latter between 7 to 12). All the survey participants were in possession of academic degrees; many of them had acquired several certifications related to the domain of agility (i.e., certified SAFe agilest, Lean Six Sigma [22] practitioner, etc.,) and they have had on-the-job training by being implicated in the implementation of software-development projects. Some candidates, on account of their long-standing experience, were directly involved in projects related to upscaling agility at a strategic level. Due to privacy reasons, the names of these respondents will not be revealed. Table 1 provides an overview of the respondents.

At a later stage, the 8 professionals received a formal email invitation along with detailed information about the interview process which would take the form of a 60-minute, individual conversation taking place using online videoconferencing. For the purposes of our study, we used a semi-structured interview format. This form of data

Table 1. Participating Respondents and Their Characteristics.

Respon-dent	Highest Degree	Current Role	Industry	Experience (in years)
R1	Master in Business Administration	Senior Consultant in Strategy and Digital Transformation for the Public Sector	Consulting	4
R2	Bachelor in Engineering	Director of Processes, Data Quality, and Innovation	Healthcare	12
R3	Master in Business and Information Systems Engineering	General Manager	IT Services and Consulting	16
R4	Master in Innovation and Entrepreneurship	Digital Transformation Manager	Consulting	6
R5	Master in Digital Product Management	IT Agile Delivery Manager	Automotive	6
R6	Master in Information Systems Management	IT Strategy Manager	Consulting	6.5
R7	Master in Business Information Management	Business Intelligence Engineer	Consulting	3
R8	Master in International Business	Information Technology Strategy Manager	Consulting	5

gathering allowed us to be in contact with the interviewees and perform an in-depth dialogue guided by a set of questions; these were meant to allow the interviewees to express their understanding of the notions of strategic and operational agility in order to identify themes, patterns, and challenges in the implementation of strategic agility. As such, these questions were meant to serve as the preamble for the examination of the StratAMoDrIGo framework by these experts. In practice, after having conducted our first interview, we went into a process of adjusting our interview protocol (i.e., some questions had to be rearranged, the focus of some questions had to be more narrow, some questions had to be dropped altogether, etc.) as the interviewees were spending too much time focusing on the thematic related to the definition and implementation of strategic agility and did not have the time to get to the part related to the examination of the StratAMoDrIGo. The interview protocol was iteratively reevaluated and readjusted three times by the research team before reaching a stable form. This fixed form was then administered to the five remaining survey participants and can be described as such: for each interviewee, a combination of open and closed questions was used; these questions were clustered around 3 major thematic areas. Each thematic successively addressed (i) the definition and distinction between operational and strategic agility, (ii) the explanation of some of the practical issues regarding the implementation of strategic agility, and (iii) the evaluation and potential applicability of StratAMoDrIGo.

3.3 Interview Protocol

The interview protocol was split into three major thematic areas (parts). The first thematic was meant to collect background information about the experts' educational accreditations, their professional engagement, as well as explicating their responsibilities under the tenure of their current role within their respective companies. However, the centerpiece of this thematic area was dedicated to inquiring how the respondents realize the notion of strategic agility (e.g., *How would you define strategic agility?., In what specific ways does strategic agility contribute to change and innovation?., According to you, what traits does an organization need to exhibit in order to achieve a state of strategic agility?., Does it have an added value in each company?* etc.,). The questions that were addressed in this cluster were also meant to capture whether the respondents are able to distinguish between the preconceptions of strategic and operational agility.

The second thematic was meant to inquire the respondents about the approaches they would take to implement strategic agility within their current role. This part was also purposed to reveal some challenges that would impede this implementation. At the same time, the respondents were asked to report what they would consider as best practice in terms of overcoming these challenges (e.g., *What do you think are the most effective methods of implementing strategic agility in a company?., Is there a standard method that you would apply in every company regardless the sector or size?., What do you consider as the biggest challenge to implement strategic agility in a company?., How do you go about in solving some of these challenges?., According to you, is there a method that offers effective tools in solving some or all of these challenges?*, etc.).

The third thematic was dedicated to the evaluation of the StratAMoDrIGo. The purpose was to provide the interviewees with a general understanding of the framework. Accordingly, the interviewer was commencing this thematic by swiftly describing (i) the general structure of the framework, and (ii) the nature of strategic opportunities and how their value-driven impact can be evaluated at a strategic-, stakeholder-, and a user-level. A set of questions were then asked to appraise whether each expert found comprehensible, valuable, functional, and practicable the attempted linkage between strategic opportunities and the pursued value-driven vistas which the framework was creating (e.g., *In what ways, if any, you think that defining strategic opportunities is important for an organization?, In what ways, if any, the definition and periodic assessment of strategic opportunities affects the achievement of strategic agility for an organization?, In what ways, if any, would the top-down governance executives/stakeholders of an organization be impacted from connecting these strategic opportunities with strategic objectives?* etc.,). The correspondence between the strategic-, and the management-layer was also being explained along with a brief illustration of the modeling approaches that were used for each layer in order to appraise (and represent) the stakeholder-, and user-level value determinants. Following, a set of questions were asked to test the respondents' understanding of the interconnection between these layers (e.g., *Do you find important to be able to produce a modeling representation between a strategic opportunity and the roles, goals, and tasks which have to be activated for the realization of this strategic opportunity?, Are there any other -or more practical- ways, methods, and/or modeling representations that you have successfully used to achieve such a level of traceability between the strategic and management level for the assessment of strategic opportunities?* etc.,). A final set of questions were meant to allow the experts freely giving their opinions regarding the structure of the framework, its corresponding parts, understandability, and ease of use.

4 Data Analysis and Results

Upon completion of the interviews, the subjects' recordings/answers were subsequently transcribed into text, analyzed, and codified which means that parts of the text were given a code representing a certain theme/construct, etc. Overall we approached the analysis of the data gathered during the interviews under the scope of thematic content analysis [2, 24]. More specifically, we revisited the recorded material several times to identify a convergence cluster within the respondents' answers which could take the form of similar phrases in different parts of the material, patterns in the data, reoccurring differences between sub-groups of subjects, etc. Data was tabulated so as to offer an overview of all main insights and themes. The results of this process are illustrated in the below tables aggregating and categorizing the responses of the interviewees in four major themes; these are correspondingly related to the interviewees' attributed strategic agility (i) definitions and characteristics (see Table 2), (ii) differentiators with operational agility (see Table 3), (iii) mode of organizational proliferation (see Table 4), and (iv) corresponding implementation patterns (see Table 5). Each one of these tables was created according to the decrees of Miles et al. [18] and Hassanzadeh et al. [12] in terms of representing qualitative interview data. Pragmatically, the first column of each tables represents the transcribed verbal statements of the interviewees; these instantiate the original verbal statements as prescribed in the interviews after being minorly processed for the sake of coherency; the meaning and general spirit of the verbal statements was not altered in any way during this process. The second column represents a codified extraction of these statements while the third column presents a theme-attribution to these codes; the codification and theme-attribution was performed jointly (and in agreement) by all the members of the research team. The final column presents the identification numbers of the interviewees (as presented in Table 1) that were attributed to the statements of the original sentences.

StratAMoDrIGo has also been audited by respondents 4 to 8 (see Table 1) in terms of its overall structure, understandability, applicability, ease of use. These experts were encouraged to consider the fit-for-use of the StratAMoDrIGo meta-model within their daily organizational activities and tasks in order to offer comments, recommendations, concerns, or vulnerabilities about its characteristics.

Regarding the framework's overall structure, all the experts seem to appreciate the trichotomy into strategic-, management-, and user-oriented layers in terms of reviewing the conceptualization of new strategic opportunities. The respondents acknowledge that StratAMoDrIGo is novel in the way it realizes the simultaneous representation of various bases of concerns; they recognized that the standard way of working usually considers one of those layers as the starting point of analysis. In particular, the *fourth respondent* mentions that, in the world of consultancy, it is always welcoming to be able to furnish to the clients any sort of representation of their strategic and operational level as well as being able to utilize a tool to study the interdependence between these two layers; in that way the leaders can easily create a mosaic where all the teams are represented and everyone can work in the same direction.

Moreover, all the respondents note that they were not aware of a conceptual modeling approach that could guide/aid them throughout their strategic agility implementation efforts. In that context, StratAMoDrIGo was perceived as a novel approach that could be used to define, model, and represent specific strategic objectives before the

Table 2. Codified Interview Data on Defining Strategic Agility and its Characteristics.

Transcribed Verbal Statements	Codified extraction of verbal statements	Theme	Interviewees
... a company being in a state of strategic agility must be in a position to be aware of what it wants to achieve in the future in view of the opportunities that arise.	Ability to create opportunities' awareness	Defining Strategic Agility	[2], [3], [4], [6], [7]
... Strategic agility should offer the business the opportunity to constantly revise its strategy to see if it is sill relevant	Propensity for periodic revaluation of strategy		
... Strategic agility should allow the incorporation and configuration of processes and/or systems in such a way that the business can quickly adapt to a changing context or environment	Capacity to incorporate processes and specific systems		
... Strategic agility is about leaders imbuing a certain time of mindset to the rest of the team. It is about having the vision to manage the company from a high-level and strategic point of view, starting from a proper value creation	Enabling thought leadership and value creation		
... Strategic agility is about being able to offer the tools so that the company can adapt to clients' constantly changing needs.	Ability to create situational awareness for client's needs.		
... Strategic agility allows for greater flexibility and encourages innovation and creativity	Flexibility	Strategic Agility characteristics	[1], [4], [6], [8]
... Strategic agility offers a company-wide approach of being flexible, adaptive and geared towards change	Innovation-driven. Adaptability		
... Strategic agility has a wider view and a longer time horizon in terms of reevaluating the core business for the achievement of objectives.	Change-oriented mentality. Extensive time horizon.		

start of a particular IT development project; these strategic objectives could be then communicated more easily with other stakeholders and create a sense of unity within the organization. The *fifth respondent* observes specifically that the 'use of models offers visibility in the attainment of organizational goals and a sense of 'story-telling' that can be propagated to the work of agile teams when performing their development. However, some reservations were expressed regarding the framework's ease-of-use and instant applicability; according to the respondent, the successful adoption of a strategic agility framework depends highly on its ability to be perceived as 'plug-and-play'. In that aspect, the fifth respondent juxtaposed StratAMoDrIGo with the SAFe framework and the latter's perceived advantage of having in its disposal a number of certified practitioners promising a quick (and standardized) deployment with an immediate return-on-investment. Therefore, the respondent believes that the StratAMoDrIGo would benefit from a customized and user-friendly interface that would convince the management level of its added value and would influence its adoption; the respondent realizes though that such an endeavor would require the framework to be applied in multiple organiza-

Table 3. Codified Interview Data on Differentiators Between Strategic and Operational Agility.

Transcribed Verbal Statements	Codified extraction of verbal statements	Theme	Interviewees
...Even though strategic agility should not be confused with operational agility within the layers of an organization, it is almost impossible to implement the former without a universal acceptance of the importance of the latter	Interdependence between strategic and operational agility	Strategic versus Operational Agility	[1], [2], [8], [3]
...Nowadays, it is not enough to focus only on operational agility. To survive companies must embrace an agile way of working at the strategic level	Upscaling operational agility at the strategic level		
...Operational agility is about simplification of structures and finding efficiency in the way teams are working together	Operational agility for efficiency, strategic agility to recognize novel opportunities		
...Operational agility is about being more efficient at what you do while strategic agility is about recognizing opportunities outside the core of your business			

Table 4. Codified Interview Data on Strategic Agility's Mode of Organizational Proliferation.

Transcribed Verbal Statements	Codified extraction of verbal statements	Theme	Interviewees
...Achieving strategic agility from all levels is better than a top-down indoctrination or an attempt for a bottom-up upscale of any operational efficiencies	Round-trip adoption of strategic agility	Choosing a top-down or a bottom-up proliferation of strategic agility	[4], [6], [7], [5], [8]
...Strategic agility should be implemented across the levels of the organization, and should not be limited to the strategic level			
...A constant emphasis on communication on all layers can facilitate the imbue of a strategic agility mentality and can give a better overview of the projects' progress and scope.	Emphasis on communication to facilitate adoption		
...however, the characteristics of a company should drive the choice between a top-down or a bottom up approach (depending on the scope, the size, and the availability of resources for an organization). For example a technical-oriented company could work faster/more efficiently by upscaling their agile ways of working.	Companies to choose an adoption plan that fits them best.		

tions (of varying sizes and sectors) and that the industry today is quite competitive (and in multiple occasions fragmented) making the exploration of new ideas quite difficult.

The *sixth* and *eighth respondents* emphasized on the framework's utilization of value streams. They reported that incorporating different value streams plays a major role in their line of business as it would allow them to create instant client satisfaction,

Table 5. Codified Interview Data on Implementation Patterns for Strategic Agility.

Transcribed Verbal Statements	Codified extraction of verbal statements	Theme	Interviewees
...The means and methods to implement strategic agility depends highly on the industry and sector of each company	No universal approach for implementing strategic agility	Imple-menting Strategic Agility	[1], [2], [3], [4], [5], [6], [7], [8]
...Companies should start by looking at their assets and decide which ones they want to keep and which ones need further development. On top of that, they must look at where they want to go and in which markets they want to be active	Define priorities and opportunities before implementation		
...It is important that the whole company understands the importance of the strategic agility implementation and stimulates the dialogue about it. Incorporating it in the annual policy and objectives ensures a uneventful implementation	Embrace strategic agility at the C-level, and allocate resources		[2], [1], [3]
...Avoiding contradictory decisions during the implementation process is crucial			
...Establish a cross-functional and complementary team ensuring that the right people support the implementation process, and allow the team to access resources for the fulfillment of their mission			
...A regular, periodic, two-way communication between the implementation team, the C-levels and the rest of the stakeholders is crucial for the success of the implementation	Establish change management processes and communicate effectively		[4], [6], [1]
...Change management and communication is key when implementing strategic agility			
...The strategic vision for the implementation should be shared throughout all the organizational layers			
...Creativity and innovation can be stimulated when companies eliminate internal bureaucracy and downtime can be minimized.	Eradicate bureaucratic procedures and hierarchical impermeability.		[1], [3]
...an ideation process having to go through many validation layers/steps does not guarantee neither an effective nor an efficient implementation			
...Big companies and organizations are much more keen to adapt the latest agile frameworks; smaller companies and start-ups try to implement strategy agility using ad-hoc techniques based on practical experience since they are on a resource-saving mode	Established companies versus SMEs and start-ups		[7], [3], [2]
...Established companies also face the danger of stop looking for opportunities once they have found a successful product or service; hence, the implementation of strategic agility may seem obsolete			
...Established companies are in a more comfortable position with a more predictable income, while start-ups really need to operate in the right market and offer the right products in order to survive. Therefore, start-ups seem to be more urged to implement strategic agility			

especially during the delivery of the first minimum viable product. Nonetheless, the sixth respondent noted that the use of certain modeling notations within the framework may seem counterintuitive and might make harder the representation of the management-level tasks and value streams; the respondent noted that it is not always easy to get professionals initiated to new modeling notations; that initiation might even backfire if it is 'forced-fed' from the top. But the respondent recognizes that teams are often unwilling to adopt a new element/technique in their way of working so StratA-MoDrIGo should be reinforced with some basic change management guidelines. The eighth respondent was also sceptic about some modeling techniques.

Finally, the *seventh respondent* recognized the added value of utilizing intentionality to model the task-to-goal dependencies at the management level and the specification of the roles that are entailed within this layer. The respondent added that, on many occasions, the middle-layer is not given enough attention as the entire focus goes either on the C-level (and the determination of strategy) or on the operational layer (and the effort to upscale their agile way of working into the wider organizational spectrum). The respondent also assessed positively the framework's round-trip (top-down and bottom-up) assessment of potential strategic opportunities from all organizational levels. The abstractive logic that StratAMoDrIGo propagates for a fast assessment of strategic opportunities was viewed positively; however, the respondent would have also liked to see a link between the StratAMoDrIGo's meta-model and the materialization of a detailed script (perhaps in the logic of a balanced scorecard) that would provide some sort of accountability for the C-level and middle-level management in terms of appropriating, in the maximum level, the strategic opportunities that arise.

5   Discussion and Conclusion

The data can yield some primary remarks: overall, the majority of the interviewees seems to be describing the notion of strategic agility by using similar (marginally distinguishable) characteristics. Indeed, our survey suggests that strategic agility is more than often associated with the ability of an organization to be in a state of openness, adaptiveness, and flexibility in order to discover opportunities outside its main business scope. This seems to be in agreement with the classic bibliographic attribution to strategic agility; for example the studies of Weber & Tara [28] and Lewis et al. [17] essentially describe strategic agility as the ability of a company to sense opportunities, to successfully respond to them and to be aware of any reoccurring business-impacting changes. Nonetheless, a closer examination of our data relinquishes some new significations: **first,** it suggests the coupling of strategic agility with the enablement of thought leadership at the top and the inculcation of a value-creation mentality to all the actors residing within the boundaries of the organizational spectrum. By no means does this observation suggest any sort of top-down tutelage but rather the interviewees seem to attribute the success of such a process to the C-level management ensuring (i) the effective incorporation of multi-channeled communication for the timely funneling and dissemination of information, (ii) the definitive prescription and propagation of strategic objectives and (iii) the set-up of an efficient resource-allocation mechanism. The aforementioned factors are perceived by the interviewees as the epitome of every proper stakeholder-management regiment that should be supporting every strategic agility implementation framework. Starting from the last point, StratAMoDrIGo does not prescribe specifically the elaboration of a definitive resource allocation mechanism by the C-level; the framework's purpose is not fixed on the detailed specification of the duties of each role within an organization as this would transgress axiomatically the notion of agility. It does, however, provide a core stakeholder-driven analysis where multiple viewpoints are being taken into consideration for the evaluation of the impact of a new (strategic) opportunity. Additionally, the majority of the interviewees seem to accede to the framework's use of visualizations as the medium of an effective communication regarding the substance of strategic objectives. There was also positive support on the framework's provided impact analysis of user-driven concerns within the shaping process of these strategic objectives. During the evaluation of StratAMoDrIGo, there were concerns expressed by some interviewees about the use of specific (and task-oriented) modeling techniques within the framework itself. However, StratAMoDrIGo is not restrictive in the use of these techniques; it does allow the use of customization in order to be compatible with the modeling formations that different teams are accustomed to.

Second, all the interviewees are able to produce a definitory distinction between operational agility and strategic agility; however, the majority of them acknowledge that most organizations are not likely to achieve the latter unless they have first established a shared culture as well as a precedent in the ways-of-working of the former. The interviewees suggest that the aptness to efficiency, the liberation from sluggish hierarchical evaluation procedures, and the empowerment of the personnel that seem to be at the forefront of many operational agility frameworks (e.g., Scrum, Kanban, etc.,) should be imbued in every strategic agility implementation mechanism. In that sense, StratAMoDrIGo's feature-driven exploration in terms of swiftly evaluating novel strategic opportunities encapsulates the essential competences as exhibited within various agile methodologies (the previous chapter mentions Scrum specifically but other methodologies can be utilized and incorporated in StratAMoDrIGo's core). Some interviewees seemed to express some concern whether a periodic alignment evaluation between (operational) user-driven features and top-down defined strategic objectives would signify a dampening of the agility effect within the entire development process.

Third, our data suggest that strategic agility seems to be associated with the structured incorporation (and/or configuration) of processes (and/or systems) that would (i) strive for a constant improvement of internal procedures, and (ii) allow the detection of even minor changes within the business habitat. The interviewees did not seem to favor the use of a specific technique, method, or modeling language for the set-up of such processes; they did, however, seem to prefer the utilization of 'plug-and-play' techniques that could provide instant insights in terms of evaluating (and optimizing) the state of organizational-wide agility. The interviewees expressed the consideration that conceptual modeling-based methods (such as StratAMoDrIGo) are deemed to require some acclimation to those with no prior experience in practicing them.

At this point, we need to be critical regarding the limitations that might have influenced our results in some manner. We acknowledge that our sampling technique, which relied mostly on a combination of convenience and snowball sampling, may have been suboptimal in terms of (i) using a specified sampling frame to monitor the representability of our population and (ii) making strong statistical inferences on that population based on the retrieved sample. Nonetheless, we used these particular sampling methods because we wanted to retrieve candidates whose roles/functions adhered to a very specific set of attributes. Given the potentially small size of the population permeating individuals with such exact characteristics, the use of non-probability sampling techniques can be justified as long as there is some caution regarding the generalization of the sample findings [25] while being attentive in curving the sampling bias. In terms of the latter, the recognition of the attributes of our population was the result of an active deliberation process amongst the members of the research team. Specifically, each team member was asked individually to create a list containing the potential characteristics of the population; following, a discussion took place based on these individual lists where the exact characteristics were determined upon unanimity amongst the team members. Furthermore, the compliance to a population with such particular characteristics accounts for the deliverance of a non-extended number for the final survey-participants. This creates an extra consideration whether the number of the interviewees could have been higher in order to reach a fuller information backlog. However, given the set time-frame of the survey process, the addition of more interviewees that would not precisely satisfy the criteria established by the research team would only harm the quality of the retrieved information. Finally, we need to note that not all interviewees got the opportunity to evaluate StratAMoDrIGo; as explained in the sections before, the information extracted by the first three interviewees was used as input in the process of the iterative build-up of our interview protocol. Therefore, although not every survey participant was given the chance to perform the framework evaluation, the information provided by the first three interviewees gave us the chance to construct an interview protocol that could frame the questions about the definition of strategic agility and the framework evaluation rather well for the remaining sample instances.

References

1. Ahammad, M.F., Glaister, K.W., Gomes, E.: Strategic agility and human resource management. Hum. Resour. Manag. Rev. **30**(1), 100700 (2020)
2. Anderson, R.: Thematic content analysis: descr. pres. of qual. data. Phd thesis (2007)
3. Benbasat, I., Goldstein, D.K., Mead, M.: The case research strategy in studies of information systems. MIS Q. **11**(3), 369–386 (1987)
4. Brown, T.A.: Confirmatory Factor Analysis for Applied Research. Guilford Publications (2015)
5. Castillo-Montoya, M.: Preparing for interview research: the interview protocol refinement framework. Qualitat. Rep. **21**(5), 811–831 (2016)
6. Doz, Y., Doz, Y.L., Kosonen, M.: Fast Strategy: How Strategic Agility Will Help You Stay Ahead of the Game. Pearson Education (2008)
7. Doz, Y.L., Kosonen, M.: Embedding strategic agility: a leadership agenda for accelerating business model renewal. Long Range Plan. **43**(2–3), 370–382 (2010)
8. Etikan, I., et al.: Comparison of convenience sampling and purposive sampling. Am. J. Theor. Appl. Stat. **5**(1), 1–4 (2016)
9. Evers, C.W., Wu, E.H.: On generalising from single case studies: epistemological reflections. J. Philos. Educ. **40**(4), 511–526 (2006)
10. Glesne, D., Pedersen, M.: Strategic agility: adapting and renewing strategic direction: an exploratory case study. Master's thesis (2020)

11. Guest, G., Namey, E., Chen, M.: A simple method to assess and report thematic saturation in qualitative research. PLoS ONE **15**(5), e0232076 (2020)
12. Hassanzadeh, Z.S., Hosseini, S.R., Honarbakhsh, F.: Study of the educational factors contributing to realization of the objectives of entrepreneurial university. Int. J. Adv. Appl. Sci **2**(10), 1–12 (2015)
13. Hennink, M., Kaiser, B.N.: Sample sizes for saturation in qualitative research: a systematic review of empirical tests. Soc. Sci. Med. 114523 (2021)
14. Ivory, S.B., Brooks, S.B.: Managing corporate sustainability with a paradoxical lens: lessons from strategic agility. J. Bus. Ethics **148**(2), 347–361 (2018)
15. Kaplan, B., Maxwell, J.A.: Qualitative research methods for evaluating computer information systems. In: Evaluating the Organizational Impact of Healthcare Information Systems. Health Informatics, pp. 30–55. Springer, New York (2005). https://doi.org/10.1007/0-387-30329-4_2
16. Knaster, R., Leffingwell, D.: SAFe 5. 0 Distilled: Achieving Business Agility with the Scaled Agile Framework. Pearson Education, Limited (2020)
17. Lewis, M.W., Andriopoulos, C., Smith, W.K.: Paradoxical leadership to enable strategic agility. Calif. Manage. Rev. **56**(3), 58–77 (2014)
18. Miles, M.B., Huberman, A.M., Saldaña, J.: Qualitative Data Analysis: A Methods Sourcebook. Sage Publications (2018)
19. Myers, M.D.: Qualitative Research in Business and Management. Sage (2019)
20. Saunders, M., Lewis, P., Thornhill, A.: Research Methods for Business Students. Pearson Education (2016)
21. Schurz, G.: Patterns of abduction. Synthese **164**(2), 201–234 (2008)
22. Snee, R.D.: Lean six sigma-getting better all the time. Intl. J. Lean Six Sigma (2010)
23. Tsilionis, K., Wautelet, Y.: A model-driven framework to support strategic agility: value-added perspective. Inf. Softw. Technol. **141**, 106734 (2022)
24. Vaismoradi, M., Jones, J., Turunen, H., Snelgrove, S.: Theme development in qualitative content analysis and thematic analysis (2016)
25. Vehovar, V., Toepoel, V., Steinmetz, S.: Non-probability sampling. In: The Sage Handbook of Survey Methods (2016)
26. Wautelet, Y.: A model-driven IT governance process based on the strategic impact evaluation of services. J. Syst. Softw. **149**, 462–475 (2019)
27. Wautelet, Y., Heng, S., Kiv, S., Kolp, M.: User-story driven development of multi-agent systems: a process fragment for agile methods. COMLAN **50**, 159–176 (2017)
28. Weber, Y., Tarba, S.Y.: Strategic agility: a state of the art introduction to the special section on strategic agility. Calif. Manage. Rev. **56**(3), 5–12 (2014)
29. Yin, R.K.: Validity and genlzn in future case study eval. Evaluation **19**(3), 321–332 (2013)
30. Yu, E., Giorgini, P., Maiden, N., Mylopoulos, J.: Social Modeling for Requirements Engineering. MIT Press (2011)

Comparing the Expressiveness of Imperative and Declarative Process Models

Nicolai Schützenmeier[✉], Stefan Jablonski, Martin Käppel,
and Lars Ackermann

Institute for Computer Science, University of Bayreuth, Bayreuth, Germany
{nicolai.schuetzenmeier,stefan.jablonski,martin.kaeppel,
lars.ackermann}@uni-bayreuth.de

Abstract. Since the advent of so-called *declarative* process modeling languages in addition to the previously known *imperative* languages, the business process management community has been confronted with a lot of new possibilities and challenges regarding modeling and interpreting business processes. In general, these declarative languages are better suited for flexible processes, i.e. processes which lead a lot of open decisions to the model executor and hence have got a relatively large amount of execution paths, whereas imperative languages are mainly used to formalize routine processes. Of course, the question arises whether a declarative or an imperative approach fits better for a specific application. In this paper we handle this issue and present a method based on automata theory, which supports the process modeler in making this decision. Furthermore, we present a comparison method which makes it possible to check given imperative and declarative process models for equality. We finally evaluate our approach by implementing a Java tool and calculating practical examples.

Keywords: Imperative Process Management · Declarative Process Management · Business Rules Modeling · Model Comparison

1 Introduction

Since about two decades process management is an established technology for structuring activities that are carried out in an organisation [2]. Traditionally, *imperative process modeling* approaches are pursued [21]. Such approaches are characterized by having to explicitly define each eligible process execution path. This restriction leads to the observation that imperative process models are well suited for processes with a limited number of alternative execution paths; otherwise process models would grow drastically and are not readable any more [11]. Nevertheless, imperative process models with a reasonably limited number of execution paths are very comprehensible [11].

With the advent of *declarative process modeling languages* [20] an alternative to imperative approaches has been available. A declarative process model is

E. Babkin et al. (Eds.): MOBA 2023, LNBIP 488, pp. 16–31, 2023.
https://doi.org/10.1007/978-3-031-45010-5_2

characterized by allowing all potential execution paths of process activities that are not explicitly forbidden. Consequently, this approach fits well to applications with a huge variability, i.e. a very high number of process execution paths is possible and also relevant. However, such approaches have a decisive drawback. Here the eligibility of execution paths is determined by specifying logical constraints that represent business rules. Per se, a logical constraint is harder to interpret than process activities that are connected by control-flow arrows like in an imperative process model. Besides, when the number of constraints is growing, the comprehensibility of declarative process models decreases drastically.

Traditionally domain experts choose an imperative approach for process modeling. As long as a process does not comprise too many alternative execution paths, this approach is effective. However, a problem arises when domain experts detect and experience more and more alternative execution paths. The imperative model is growing steadily and its comprehensibility is equally diminishing. At this point the question, whether to switch to a declarative modeling language, arises. Hence, automatically derived measures from the process model, which indicate whether an imperative or a declarative approach fits better for the underlying process, are needed. In case of switching the modeling language, the domain expert is confronted with the following questions:

– Does the newly developed declarative process model coincide with the formerly developed imperative model? Alternatively, is it an extension of the former model?
– If they are not equal, how far do they differ?

Since experience in declarative process modeling is still not very common and declarative process models are generally harder to interpret, these questions are not to be answered trivially.

In this paper, we address a critical challenge by offering a comprehensive solution. We present a methodology for comparing imperative and declarative process models, complete with measurements that determine the degree of similarity between them. Additionally, we leverage these measurements as indicators to help determine whether transitioning to a declarative language is advisable or not.

This paper is structured as follows. Basic terminology is introduced in Sect. 2. Related work is discussed in Sect. 3. Afterwards, it is depicted how imperative and declarative process models can be compared (Sect. 4) and how our method is implemented (Sect. 5). An experimental evaluation (Sect. 6) completes the contribution of this paper.

2   Basic Terminology and Running Examples

In this section we recall basic process management terminology, i.e. events and traces. Events and traces are needed since they form the basis of the comparison of process models stemming from both imperative and declarative process modeling languages. Two prominent representatives of those modeling approaches, i.e. BPMN and Declare, are also introduced in this section. For comparing imperative and declarative process models they have to be transformed into finite state automatons in order to define a common representation. Section 2.4 provides a short introduction to such automatons.

2.1 Events and Traces

When a process instance - which is an instantiation of a process model - is executed, this execution is recorded in a process log. There we encounter events and traces. We briefly recall the standard definitions for those concepts [2].

Definition 1. *An event is an occurrence of an activity (i.e. a well-defined step in a business process) in a particular process instance.*

Definition 2. *A **trace** is a finite sequence $\sigma = \langle e_1, ..., e_n \rangle$ such that all events belong to the same process instance and are ordered by their execution time, where $n := |\sigma|$ denotes the **trace length** of σ. We use the notation $\sigma(i)$ to refer to the i-th element in σ.*

2.2 Imperative Process Modeling and BPMN

There are two approaches for process modeling: imperative and declarative process modeling. *Imperative* process modeling is characterized by explicitly modeling each execution path that is eligible to be performed. This way of modeling is mostly used for so-called *routine* processes of which we know all eligible execution paths and their number is rather limited.

A very popular imperative process modeling language is *Business Process Model and Notation (BPMN)*.[1] In the following we give a short introduction of BPMN since we focus on this language as a representative of the imperative modeling paradigm in this paper.

Definition 3. *A **BPMN process model** is a tuple $P = (F, E, E^s, E^e, A, G, G^p, G^e, T)$ where*

- *F is a finite set of flow objects which can be partitioned into events E, activities A and gateways G,*
- *E is a finite set of events which can be partitioned into start events E^s and end events E^e,*
- *A is a finite set of activities,*
- *G is a finite set of gateways which can be partitioned into exclusive gateways G^e and parallel gateways G^p,*
- *$T \subseteq F \times F$ is a finite set of transitions.*

Note that our definition of a BPMN model only includes the core elements of BPMN because we only consider the control-flow and therefore these core elements are sufficient. All other BPMN elements are neglected in this definition

---

[1] http://www.omg.org/spec/BPMN/2.0

and in this paper. Just to focus the control-flow of a process is a very common approach and is pursued by many related approaches [17].

Figure 1 shows the graphical representation of a BPMN model P_1 which contains four *activities* A, B and C twice (represented by rectangles with rounded corners), two *exclusive gateways* (represented by diamonds filled with an X), a *start* and an *end event* (represented by [thin/thick] circles) and *transitions* between the elements (represented by arrows).

P_1 describes a process where either the three activities A, B and C are sequentially executed (i.e. ABC) or alternatively C is executed. Both alternatives must be performed at least once and can be repeated arbitrarily often. For instance, the following traces are accepted: $\langle C \rangle$, $\langle ABC \rangle$, $\langle CABC \rangle$, $\langle CC \rangle$, $\langle ABCC \rangle$, ...

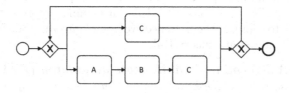

Fig. 1. BPMN model P_1.

2.3 Declarative Process Modeling and Declare

In contrast to imperative process models, *declarative* process models are interpreted in the following way: all execution paths that do not conflict with rules of a declarative process model are allowed. This results in a large number of eligible execution paths and that is why such process models are called flexible.

Declare is a well-known declarative process modeling language [20]. A Declare process model consists of a set of constraints that must be satisfied during process execution. Constraints, in turn, are instances of predefined *templates* whose semantics are formalized by the use of Linear Temporal Logic over finite traces (LTL_f) [18]. For an overview of all Declare templates see [20]. We now provide a formal definition of a Declare process model:

Definition 4. *A **Declare process model** is a pair $P = (A, T)$ where A is a finite set of activities and T is a finite set of LTL constraints.*

Figure 2 shows on the left side the graphical ConDec [19] representation of a Declare model P_2 containing three activities $A, B,$ and C and four templates which define constraints between the activities. The right side of Fig. 2 shows an equivalent textual representation P_2.

chainResponse(A,B) demands that after the execution of activity A, activity B has to be executed directly, i.e. as a next process step. *respondedExistence(A,B)* implies the occurrence of B if activity A is executed, i.e. B has to be executed before or after A. *succession(A,B)* means that the execution of A implies the execution of B afterwards and B cannot be executed if A has not been executed before. For instance, the following traces are accepted: $\langle C \rangle$, $\langle CC \rangle$, $\langle ABC \rangle$.

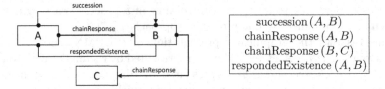

Fig. 2. Graphical ConDec representation (left) and equivalent textual representation (right) of Declare model P_2.

2.4 Automata Theory

We aim at transforming imperative and declarative process models into finite state automatons (FSAs) in order to define a common representation, which makes it possible to compare them. Hence, we briefly introduce the basic concepts and algorithms of automata theory [14].

Definition 5. *A **deterministic finite-state automaton (FSA)** is a quintuple $M = (\Sigma, S, s_0, \delta, F)$ where Σ is a finite (non-empty) set of symbols, S is a finite (non-empty) set of states, $s_0 \in S$ is an initial state, $\delta : S \times \Sigma \to S$ is the state-transition function, and $F \subseteq S$ is the set of final states.*

We do not only want to know which state transition will take place for a certain input symbol. We are more interested to know which sequences of inputs lead to state transitions that eventually end in a final state. We call such a sequence of inputs *word*, and the set of all such words is called *language* of a FSA:

Definition 6. *For a FSA $M = (\Sigma, S, s_0, \delta, F)$ we define the **extended state-transition function** $\hat\delta : S \times \Sigma^* \to S$,*

$$(s, \omega) \mapsto \begin{cases} s & \omega = \varepsilon \\ \delta(s, \omega) & \omega \in \Sigma \\ \delta(\hat\delta(s, a), b) & \omega = ab \text{ with } a \in \Sigma \text{ and } b \in \Sigma^* \end{cases}$$

where ε denotes the empty word and $\Sigma^* := \{a_1 a_2 \ldots a_n \mid n \in \mathbb{N}_0, a_i \in \Sigma\}$ denotes the set of all words over symbols in Σ.

*The set $\mathcal{L}(M) := \{\omega \in \Sigma^* \mid \hat\delta(\omega) \in F\}$ is called the **language of** M.*

Consider for example $\Sigma = \{A, B\}$. Then $\Sigma^* = \{\varepsilon, A, B, AA, AB, BA, BB, \ldots\}$ consists of all words including any number of As and Bs. The set $L := \{A\omega \mid \omega \in \Sigma^*\} = \{A, AA, AB, AAA, \ldots\}$ is the language of all words with A at the beginning. The corresponding FSA is depicted in Fig. 3. Note that the initial input B leads to a transition to state q_2 which is not a final state. Only the initial input A leads to a transition to state q_1 which is a final state (double lined circle).

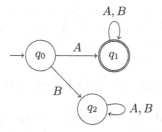

Fig. 3. Finite state automaton M with $\mathcal{L}(M) = \{A\omega \mid \omega \in \{A, B\}^*\}$.

3   Related Work

Working out coincidences of process models is a challenging task in industry and research [1,5]. One focus of this endeavor lies in comparison and aims at identifying duplicated process models in repositories or process model variants [16]. Another focus is correctness and aims at verifying transformations of process models between different modeling languages [3] and supporting the theoretical correctness of process models [4,22].

Current approaches can be partitioned into approaches to imperative process modeling languages and to declarative process modeling languages. Whereas there is a large amount of different approaches for imperative process modeling languages [10], there is only a small number of methods for declarative process models. The study in [11] reveals that single declarative process constraints can be analysed well, whereas sets of declarative constraints impose major problems, which is certainly a reason for this deficiency. Nevertheless, there are some efforts for declarative languages. The authors in [23,24] present an approach to check Declare process models for equality by using automata theory. [8] investigates incorrect Declare models in order to find inconsistencies and to fix them. In [7] an automaton-based approach is presented for the detection of redundant constraints and contradictions between constraints. [9] deals with the problem of hidden dependencies in declarative process models. Quite often all traces up to a given length are simulated in order to get a better understanding of the model and to detect possible deadlocks [15].

Due to the missing approaches to declarative process languages, there is almost no approach to model comparison of imperative and declarative process models. [21] compares the imperative and declarative modeling paradigm in general on a very abstract level, which does not help when the expressiveness of concrete process models must be examined. In [12] the authors define the equality between two process models (regardless whether they are imperative or declarative) on the base of all viable process execution paths leaving open how to handle the issue of potentially infinite sets of traces. However, the latter is an obvious feature of declarative process models and therefore must be coped with.

In summary, the need for a generally applicable method to compare imperative and declarative process models is still urgent and remains an open issue in process management research.

4   Comparing Imperative and Declarative Process Models

To compare imperative and declarative process models, such models have to be made comparable first. Thus, we transform declarative process models (Declare, Sect. 4.1) and imperative process models (BPMN, Sect. 4.2) into finite state automatons, respectively. Section 4.3 depicts our method to compare these process models after that. Finally, in Sect. 4.4 we provide a measure which supports the modeler in deciding whether a declarative or an imperative process model is better suited for the underlying process and present a measurement for the similarity of these two process models.

4.1   Transformation of Declare Models to Finite State Automatons

In order to transform a Declare model $P = (A, T)$ into a FSA, we first of all transform each Declare constraint $\tau \in T$ to a finite state automaton M_τ [24,25]. In this automaton the alphabet consists of the activities of the process and the accepted words represent all valid traces. Such an automaton accepts exactly those words whose corresponding traces are not forbidden by the corresponding constraint:

$$M_\tau \text{ accepts } \omega \iff \omega \text{ is not forbidden by } \tau.$$

In general, a Declare model consists of more than one constraint. Hence, we have to construct an automaton that represents the conjunction of all constraints. The *product automaton* [14] exactly fulfills this issue:

Definition 7. *Let* $M_1 = (\Sigma, S_1, s_{0_1}, \delta_1, F_1)$ *and* $M_2 = (\Sigma, S_2, s_{0_2}, \delta_2, F_2)$ *two deterministic finite-state automatons over the same alphabet* Σ. *The product automaton* $M = M_1 \times M_2$ *is defined as the quintuple* $M := (\Sigma, S_M, s_{0_M}, \delta_M, F_M)$ *where* $S_M = S_1 \times S_2$, $s_{0_M} = (s_{0_1}, s_{0_2})$, $\delta_M : S \times \Sigma \to S, ((s_1, s_2), a) \mapsto (\delta_1(s_1, a), \delta_2(s_2, a))$, *and* $F_M = F_1 \times F_2$.

According to the above definition, the product automaton M_T - composed of all automatons M_τ - represents a Declare process model:

$$M_T := \prod_{\tau \in T} M_\tau \text{ accepts } \omega \iff \omega \text{ is not forbidden by each } \tau \in T.$$

The transformation of a Declare model to its representing process automaton is illustrated in Algorithm 1. In order to potentially decrease the number of states of the product automaton, we use the Hopcroft minimization algorithm [14]. This minimization algorithm does not change the effectiveness of our approach and just helps to decrease the number of states.

Algorithm 1: *calculateDeclareProcessAutomaton*

Input: Declare Process Model $M = (A, \mathcal{T})$
Output: Automaton P representing M

1 $U \leftarrow \emptyset, i \leftarrow 1$
2 **for** $t \in \mathcal{T}$ **do**
3   $\quad (A, S_t, s_{0_t}, \delta_t, F_t) \leftarrow$ transform t into finite state automaton
4   $\quad t_i \leftarrow (A, S_t, s_{0_t}, \delta_t, F_t)$
5   $\quad U \leftarrow U.\text{add}(t_i)$
6   $\quad i \leftarrow i + 1$
7 **end**
8 **for** $j = 1, \dots, i - 1$ **do**
9   $\quad t_{j+1} \leftarrow \text{minimization}(\text{product}(t_j, t_{j+1}))$
    $\quad$ /* using minimization algorithm [14]   */
10 **end**
11 $P \leftarrow t_{j+1}$
12 **return** P

4.2 Transformation of BPMN Models to Finite State Automatons

We assume that BPMN models $P = (F, E, E^s, E^e, A, G, G^p, G^e, T)$ which are to be translated to finite state automatons are *well-formed* [17]. The transformation begins with the start event. Next, the constructs of a process model are transformed according to the following rules (Fig. 4):

- each sequence of n activities is mapped to a FSA with $n + 1$ states combined by transitions labeled with the activity names (Fig. 4, upper part)
- the alternative paths of an exclusive gateway are mapped to two state transitions labeled by the respective activities (Fig. 4, middle part)
- the paths of a parallel gateway are mapped to two pairs of state transitions composed by the activities of the parallel paths (Fig. 4, lower part)

Iteratively, the generated FSAs are concatenated. The dotted transitions and states in Fig. 4 indicate the melting spot for subsequent FSAs. We denote the procedure of converting a BPMN diagram to a FSA by *calculateBPMNProcessAutomaton*.

4.3 Comparing Process Models

After having transformed a Declare and a well-formed BPMN process model to finite state automatons $M_1 = (A_1, S_1, s_{0_1}, \delta_1, F_1)$ and $M_2 = (A_2, S_2, s_{0_2}, \delta_2, F_2)$ (Sects. 4.1 and 4.2), we can check the process models for equality. Therefore, we are going to calculate a variant of the product automaton of M_1 and M_2. Since the two process models might comprise different activities, i.e. the corresponding FSAs show different inputs ($A_1 \neq A_2$), we expand them by $\omega \in A_j \setminus A_i$, respectively, to achieve a common input alphabet. This is done by adding a new state s_{f_i} to S_i with a transition from each state $s \in S_i$ to s_{f_i} for each activity

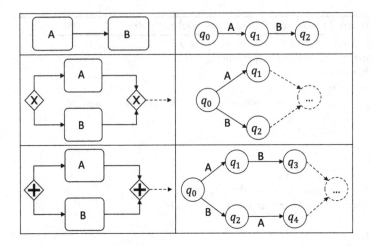

Fig. 4. Transformation rules for basic BPMN constructs.

Algorithm 2: *expandFiniteStateAutomaton*

Input: Finite state automaton $M = (\Sigma_1, S, s_0, \delta, F)$, set of symbols Σ_2
Output: Expanded finite state automaton $M_e = (\Sigma_1 \cup \Sigma_2, S, s_0, \delta_e, F)$

1 **for** $\omega \in \Sigma_2$ **do**
2   **if** $\Sigma_2 \setminus \Sigma_1 \neq \emptyset$ **then**
3        $S.\text{add}(s_f)$
4   **for** $\omega \in \Sigma_2 \setminus \Sigma_1$ **do**
5   **for** $s \in S$ **do**
6   add transition from s to s_f
7   **end**
8   **end**
9   **end**
10   **for** $\omega \in \Sigma_1 \setminus \Sigma_2$ **do**
11   add transition from s_f to s_f
12   **end**
13 **end**
14 **return** $M_e = (\Sigma_1 \cup \Sigma_2, S, s_0, \delta_e, F)$

$\omega \in A_j \setminus A_i$. For each activity $\omega \in A_1 \cup A_2$, a reflexive transition from state s_{f_i} leads into itself (Algorithm 2).

After calculating the expanded finite state automatons M_1' and M_2' of M_1 and M_2, we calculate an automaton M_s for the *symmetric difference* between M_1' and M_2'. This automaton accepts the input $\{\omega \in \Sigma_1 \cup \Sigma_2 \mid \omega \notin \Sigma_1 \cap \Sigma_2\}$. The way of constructing this automaton is similar to the above construction of the product automaton and only differs in the set of accepting states: a state of the automaton for the symmetric difference is an accepting state if and only if exactly one of the originally states of M_1' and M_2' is an accepting state (and not both as for the product automaton) [14]. The calculated automaton M_s for the symmetric difference of M_1' and M_2' has the following property:

M_s does not have an accepting state $\iff M_1'$ and M_2' accept the same language.

Hence, the two process models P_1 and P_2 are equal iff the constructed automaton for the symmetric difference does not have an accepting state. Algorithm 3 shows the complete process of checking two models for equality.

Algorithm 3: *checkForEquality*

Input: Declare Process Model $P_1 = (A_1, \mathcal{T})$, BPMN process model P_2
Output: **true**, if models are equal; **false** otherwise
1   $M_1 := (A_1, S_1, s_{0_1}, \delta_1, F_1) \leftarrow calculateDeclareProcessAutomaton(P_1)$
2   $M_2 := (A_2, S_2, s_{0_2}, \delta_2, F_2) \leftarrow calculateBPMNProcessAutomaton(P_2)$
3   $M_1' \leftarrow expandFiniteStateAutomaton(M_1, A_2)$
4   $M_2' \leftarrow expandFiniteStateAutomaton(M_2, A_1)$
5   $M_s := (A_1 \cup A_2, S_s, S_{0_s}, \delta_s, F_s) \leftarrow symmetricDifference(M_1', M_2')$
6   **if** $F_s = \emptyset$ **then**
7 | return **true**
8   **else**
9 | return **false**
10 **end**

4.4 Similarity of Process Models

The similarity of (imperative and declarative) process models is an important research question [4]. Tightly coupled with this question is the issue whether an imperative or a declarative modeling approach fits better to a certain application scenario. In order to answer these questions, we assume that in real process executions, the number of executed process steps is limited (otherwise process executions would be endless). Hence, when comparing process models, we do so with respect to specifically given trace lengths and, therefore, provide relative answers. This is firstly practically justified and secondly makes it possible to implement an application of our theoretical framework (Sect. 5).

For a given trace length n over m different activities, there are m^n theoretical traces. Now we can define the n-**density** of a process model:

Definition 8. *For a process model P over m activities we call*

$$\lambda_n(P) := \frac{|\{\sigma \text{ of length } n \mid \sigma \text{ valid trace of } P\}|}{m^n} \in [0, 1]$$

*the n-**density** of P.*

As $\{\sigma$ of length $n \mid \sigma$ valid trace of $P\}$ is a subset of all traces of length n, $\lambda_n(P)$ takes a value between 0 and 1. So $\lambda_n(P)$ describes the percentage of traces of length n which are valid traces of P. The higher the n-density, the more eligible traces of length n. This implies more flexibility in process execution and thus indicates that a declarative process approach might be more appropriate. Due to our experience in process modeling, we refrain from setting an exact threshold between the usage of an imperative and a declarative process model, but regard this observation as foundation of a decent discussion of this issue.

In case that an imperative and a declarative process model are unequal, it is interesting to know how far they differ. One way of measuring the similarity of two models P_1 and P_2 is to compare the corresponding n-densities. If the values differ extremely, P_1 and P_2 cannot have a lot of properties in common. If $\lambda_n(P_1) = d_1$ and $\lambda_n(P_2) = d_2$ and $d_1 < d_2$, they coincide in at most d_1 percent of all traces and they differ in at least $d_2 - d_1$ percentage of all traces. Note that a similar n-density does not necessarily mean that the models are similar. Even in the case $\lambda_n(P_1) = 0.5 = \lambda_n(P_2)$, it could be possible that the sets of accepted traces of the two models are completely disjoint. As a consequence, n-density should only be used to make statements about inequality of models.

Another method for measuring the similarity of two process models is n-*similarity*:

Definition 9. *For two process models P_1 and P_2 we call*

$$\Lambda_n(P_1, P_2) := \min_{j \in \{1,2\}} \left\{ \frac{|\{\sigma \text{ of length } n \mid \sigma \text{ valid trace of } P_1 \text{ and } P_2\}|}{|\{\sigma \text{ of length } n \mid \sigma \text{ valid trace of } P_j\}|} \right\} \in [0, 1]$$

*the n -**similarity** of P_1 and P_2.*

The measure of n-similarity determines the percentage of traces which are accepted by both models. Consider, for example, that P_1 accepts 100 traces of length n, P_2 accepts 200 traces of length n and the set of traces of length n which both models accept consists of 50 traces. Then $\Lambda_n(P_1, P_2) = \min\{\frac{50}{100}, \frac{50}{200}\} = 0.25$. This means that 25 percent of the traces of the more flexible model (i.e. the model which accepts more traces) are accepted by both models.

5   Implementation

In preparation for an experimental evaluation, the algorithms defined in Sect. 4 have been implemented as a Java application that provides a concise command-line interface. All sources and sample models are available online.[2]

The tool is organized as an end-to-end pipeline taking two models and configuration parameters as input and returning a binary equality decision for the provided models. Each of the models can be either a BPMN or a Declare model as long as it conforms to a predefined format (see the GitHub repository for more information on formats). Supported optional configuration parameters are:

---

[2] https://github.com/NicolaiSchuetzenmeier/Compare-BPMN-Declare

–dfa-output: If used, also the generated FSAs are returned.
–max-word-length: A positive value that determines the maximum trace length used for checking the equality of the two models (if not provided, a default value is used).
–list-constraints: Lists all supported Declare constraints.
–help: Provides information about how to use the command-line interface.

Additionally, it is possible to generate all valid words/traces up to *max-word-length* for a single given model using the option *--language-output*.

6   Experimental Evaluation

For the evaluation of our approach, we perform the following experiment. We take two process models, an imperative one and a declarative one, at a time and check them for equality. If they are not equal, we calculate the measures introduced in Sect. 4.4 and provide a pragmatic interpretation of this dissimilarity.

Example 1. As a first example we compare the two process models introduced in Sects. 2.2 and 2.3, respectively. The BPMN process model P_1 (Fig. 1) and the Declare process model P_2 (Fig. 2) both comprise the same set of activities A, B, and C. The application of the transformation methods of Sects. 4.2 and 4.1 results in the process automatons D_1 and D_2 depicted in Fig. 5.

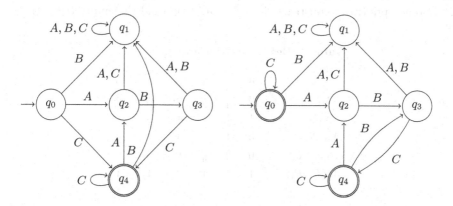

Fig. 5. Process automatons D_1 for P_1 (left) and D_2 for P_2 (right).

As P_1 and P_2 comprise the same set of activities, the automatons do not have to be expanded as discussed in Sect. 4.3. The two automatons in Fig. 5 reveal clearly that D_1 and D_2 do not accept the same language. For example, D_1 does not accept the empty word ε whereas D_2 does. Hence, the underlying process models P_1 and P_2 are not equivalent. Indeed, calculating the symmetric difference of D_1 and D_2 (Sect. 4.3) leads to the same result, i.e. the corresponding

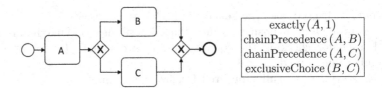

Fig. 6. BPMN model P_3 and Declare model P_4.

automaton has accepting states. Besides ε, the input $ABCBC$ is accepted by the right automaton but not by the left one. It is also accepted by the automaton for the symmetric difference.

In order to determine how far P_1 and P_2 differ, we assemble the measures as introduced in Sect. 4.4 in Table 1. The relatively small n-densities ($\lambda_n(P_i)$) recommend an imperative modeling approach. The only word of length 0, the empty word ε, is only accepted by P_2. Hence, the 0-similarity between P_1 and P_2 is 0, i.e. $\Lambda_0(M_1, M_2) = 0$. We observe that $\Lambda_n(M_1, M_2) = 1$ for $n = 1, 2, 3, 4$. This means that both models coincide for these trace lengths. Exactly these traces are accepted by both process models: $\{C, CC, CCC, ABC, CCCC, ABCC, CABC\}$. For $n = 5$ P_1 and P_2 differ in one accepted trace: $\langle ABCBC \rangle$ is accepted by P_2 but not by P_1. For $n > 5$ we derive from the automatons that there are two different loops for the word construction: the sequence ABC can be run in both models starting in state q_4. For process P_2 there is another loop BC between q_4 and q_3. Overall, each trace accepted by P_1 is also accepted by P_2. In addition, P_2 also accepts traces constructed by the BC loop (and the empty trace ε).

Table 1. Density and similarity measures.

n	0	1	2	3	4	5
$\lambda_n(P_1)$	0	$\frac{1}{3}$	$\frac{1}{9}$	$\frac{2}{27}$	$\frac{1}{27}$	$\frac{4}{243}$
$\lambda_n(P_2)$	1	$\frac{1}{3}$	$\frac{1}{9}$	$\frac{2}{27}$	$\frac{1}{27}$	$\frac{5}{243}$
$\Lambda_n(P_1, P_2)$	0	1	1	1	1	$\frac{4}{5}$
$\lambda_n(P_3) = \lambda_n(P_4)$	0	0	$\frac{2}{9}$	0	0	0
$\Lambda_n(P_3, P_4)$	1	1	1	1	1	1

Example 2. As a second example we first consider the BPMN model P_3 illustrated on the left side of Fig. 6. This model offers only two execution paths: AB and AC. This imperative process model will finally be compared with the Declare model P_4 on the right side of Fig. 6. P_4 consists of four constraints.

Calculating the process automatons D_3 and D_4 for the models P_3 and P_4 results in the same automaton (Fig. 7). Hence, P_3 and P_4 represent the same process, i.e. they accept the same set of traces.

As P_3 and P_4 only accept the same two traces of length 2, the n-densities are 0 for all $n \neq 2$, and $\frac{2}{9}$ for $n = 2$ (Table 1). Consequently, an imperative approach is suited much better for this process, since the number of eligible process paths is very limited. It is obvious that $\Lambda_n(P_3, P_4) = 1$ for all $n \in \mathbb{N}$ because $P_3 = P_4$, i.e. both process models accept the same traces.

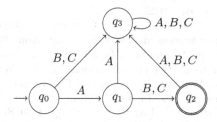

Fig. 7. Process automaton $D_3 = D_4$ for P_3 and P_4.

7   Conclusion and Future Work

In this paper we presented an approach to comparing imperative and declarative process models. Therefore, the models to be examined are converted to finite state automatons. Using standard automata theory, statements about equivalence of process models can be made. We further defined measures in order to get hints whether an imperative or a declarative approach fits better for a specific issue. Finally, we fostered statements about how far two unequal models differ.

In future work, our approach will be extended to other process modeling languages like DCR graphs [13] and especially to so-called multi-perspective languages like MP-Declare [6]. Whereas Declare mainly considers the control-flow-perspective [2], MP-Declare can also deal with human and technical resources like performing actors or used artifacts (e.g. computer programs, tools).

References

1. van der Aalst, W.M.P., de Medeiros, A.K.A., Weijters, A.J.M.M.: Process equivalence: comparing two process models based on observed behavior. In: Dustdar, S., Fiadeiro, J.L., Sheth, A.P. (eds.) BPM 2006. LNCS, vol. 4102, pp. 129–144. Springer, Heidelberg (2006). https://doi.org/10.1007/11841760_10
2. van der Aalst, W.M.P.: Process Mining - Discovery, Conformance and Enhancement of Business Processes. Springer, Wiesbaden (2011). https://doi.org/10.1007/978-3-642-19345-3
3. Ackermann, L., Schönig, S., Jablonski, S.: Towards simulation- and mining-based translation of process models. In: Pergl, R., Molhanec, M., Babkin, E., Fosso Wamba, S. (eds.) Enterprise and Organizational Modeling and Simulation, EOMAS 2016. LNBIP, vol. 272. Springer, Cham (2016). https://doi.org/10.1007/978-3-319-49454-8_1

4. Aiolli, F., Burattin, A., Sperduti, A.: A business process metric based on the alpha algorithm relations. In: Daniel, F., Barkaoui, K., Dustdar, S. (eds.) BPM 2011. LNBIP, vol. 99, pp. 141–146. Springer, Heidelberg (2012). https://doi.org/10.1007/978-3-642-28108-2_13

5. Becker, M., Laue, R.: A comparative survey of business process similarity measures. Comput. Ind. **63**, 148–167 (2012)

6. Burattin, A., Maggi, F.M., Sperduti, A.: Conformance checking based on multi-perspective declarative process models. Expert Syst. Appl. **65**, 194–211 (2016)

7. Ciccio, C.D., Maggi, F.M., Montali, M., Mendling, J.: Resolving inconsistencies and redundancies in declarative process models. Inf. Syst. **64**, 425–446 (2017)

8. Corea, C., Nagel, S., Mendling, J., Delfmann, P.: Interactive and minimal repair of declarative process models. In: Polyvyanyy, A., Wynn, M.T., Van Looy, A., Reichert, M. (eds.) BPM 2021. LNBIP, vol. 427, pp. 3–19. Springer, Cham (2021). https://doi.org/10.1007/978-3-030-85440-9_1

9. De Smedt, J., De Weerdt, J., Serral, E., Vanthienen, J.: Improving understandability of declarative process models by revealing hidden dependencies. In: Nurcan, S., Soffer, P., Bajec, M., Eder, J. (eds.) CAiSE 2016. LNCS, vol. 9694, pp. 83–98. Springer, Cham (2016). https://doi.org/10.1007/978-3-319-39696-5_6

10. Dijkman, R., Dumas, M., van Dongen, B., Käärik, R., Mendling, J.: Similarity of business process models: metrics and evaluation. Inf. Syst. **36**(2), 498–516 (2011). Special Issue: Semantic Integration of Data, Multimedia, and Services

11. Haisjackl, C., et al.: Understanding declare models: strategies, pitfalls, empirical results. Softw. Syst. Model. **15**(2), 325–352 (2016)

12. Hidders, J., Dumas, M., van der Aalst, W.M.P., ter Hofstede, A.H.M., Verelst, J.: When are two workflows the same? In: Proceedings of the 2005 Australasian Symposium on Theory of Computing, vol. 41, pp. 3–11. AUS (2005)

13. Hildebrandt, T.T., Mukkamala, R.R., Slaats, T., Zanitti, F.: Contracts for cross-organizational workflows as timed dynamic condition response graphs. J. Log. Algebr. Program. **82**(5–7), 164–185 (2013)

14. Hopcroft, J., Motwani, R., Ullman, J.: Introduction to Automata Theory, Languages, and Computation. Pearson/Addison Wesley, New York (2007)

15. Käppel, M., Schützenmeier, N., Schönig, S., Ackermann, L., Jablonski, S.: Logic based look-ahead for the execution of multi-perspective declarative processes. In: Reinhartz-Berger, I., Zdravkovic, J., Gulden, J., Schmidt, R. (eds.) BPMDS/EMMSAD -2019. LNBIP, vol. 352, pp. 53–68. Springer, Cham (2019). https://doi.org/10.1007/978-3-030-20618-5_4

16. La Rosa, M., Dumas, M., Ekanayake, C., García-Bañuelos, L., Recker, J., Hofstede, A.: Detecting approximate clones in business process model repositories. Inf. Syst. **49**, 102–125 (2015)

17. Mahleko, B., Wombacher, A.: Indexing business processes based on annotated finite state automata. In: IEEE International Conference on Web Services (2006)

18. Montali, M., Pesic, M., van der Aalst, W.M.P., Chesani, F., Mello, P., Storari, S.: Declarative specification and verification of service choreographies. ACM Trans. Web **4**(1), 1–62 (2010)

19. Pesic, M., van der Aalst, W.M.P.: A declarative approach for flexible business processes management. In: Eder, J., Dustdar, S. (eds.) BPM 2006. LNCS, vol. 4103, pp. 169–180. Springer, Heidelberg (2006). https://doi.org/10.1007/11837862_18

20. Pesic, M., Schonenberg, H., Aalst, W.: Declare: full support for loosely-structured processes. In: Proceedings - IEEE International Enterprise Distributed Object Computing Workshop, EDOC, p. 287, November 2007

21. Pichler, P., Weber, B., Zugal, S., Pinggera, J., Mendling, J., Reijers, H.: Imperative versus declarative process modeling languages: an empirical investigation. In: Business Process Management Workshops, vol. 99, pp. 383–394, August 2011
22. Schützenmeier., N., Käppel., M., Fichtner., M., Jablonski., S.: Scenario-based model checking of declarative process models. In: Proceedings of the 25th International Conference on Enterprise Information Systems. SciTePress (2023)
23. Schützenmeier, N., Käppel, M., Ackermann, L., Jablonski, S., Petter, S.: Automaton-based comparison of declare process models. Softw. Syst. Model. **22**, 667–685 (2022)
24. Schützenmeier, N., Käppel, M., Petter, S., Jablonski, S.: Upper-bounded model checking for declarative process models. In: Serral, E., Stirna, J., Ralyté, J., Grabis, J. (eds.) PoEM 2021. LNBIP, vol. 432, pp. 195–211. Springer, Cham (2021). https://doi.org/10.1007/978-3-030-91279-6_14
25. Westergaard, M., Stahl, C., Reijers, H.: UnconstrainedMiner: efficient discovery of generalized declarative process models. BPMcenter.org BPM reports (2013)

Deriving Relational Normalisation from Conceptual Normalisation

Martin Molhanec[✉] [iD]

Czech Technical University in Prague, Prague, Czech Republic
molhanec@fel.cvut.cz

Abstract. This article argues that relational normalisation can be derived from conceptual normalisation. First, relational normalisation, which is widely known, is introduced. Furthermore, the conceptual normalisation presented by the Author in his previous articles is presented. Finally, the Author shows how relational normalisation can be derived from conceptual normalisation. In the end, the Author outlines the further possible development of his work in this area.

Keywords: Data Normalisation · Conceptual Normal Forms · Relational Normal Forms

1 Introduction

This article deals with the issue of deriving relational normalisation from conceptual normalisation. The Author has been dealing with this issue for many years and has published his ideas in previous years, for example, at the international workshop EOMAS [1–3] and the ISD (Information System Development) Conference [4]. So, this article is among many others that disseminate the Author's views more widely to the international conceptual and data modelling expert community. The Author hopes this paper can be a good starting point for further discussing these interesting theoretical issues.

The remainder of this document is organised as follows. In Sect. 2, we will start with what motivates us, i.e., why it is interesting to derive relational normalisation from conceptual normalisation. Section 3 presents our assumptions and approach. After that, Sect. 4 presents the results of our work, i.e., the actual derivation of relational normalisation from conceptual normalisation. Finally, Sect. 5 summarises the paper, suggests improvements, and discusses future research directions.

2 Motivation and Problem Statement

The principle of relational normalisation (1st to 3rd normal forms and others that are not so common, such as BNCF) is commonly taught in database theory and design university courses. Its usefulness and suitability cannot be doubted. From the rich literature, we can refer here, for example, to the works of the founder of the theory of database systems, Edgar F. Codd [5–7]. However, the Author of this paper feels that the basic postulates of relational normalisation can be better established by deriving them from conceptual normalisation, which he will try to prove in this article.

E. Babkin et al. (Eds.): MOBA 2023, LNBIP 488, pp. 32–41, 2023.
https://doi.org/10.1007/978-3-031-45010-5_3

Issues of proper design of data models have been discussed as early as the 1970 s, starting with the well-known article by Chen [8]. The fact-based modelling approach also gives special attention to this issue; see [9] and [10]. The Author's approach is based on ontology theory and conceptual modelling paradigm.

We argue that the need for relational normalisation arises for the same reasons as for conceptual normalisation, i.e., the need to eliminate redundancy from our data. Using primary and foreign keys in relational normalisation definitions is a way to implement conceptual normalisation for relational databases. In this way, the definitions of the relational normal forms follow directly from the definitions of the conceptual normal forms.

3 Presumptions and Our Approach

3.1 Conceptual Normal Forms (CNFs)

We begin this section with the following statement, in our opinion, the basic assumption is that the relational and object models are specialisations of a more general conceptual model based on the ontology of the Real World, which is a higher-level model, and that these models are not subtypes of each other.

For this reason, we defend our claim that relational and object normalisation are specialisations of the much more general conceptual normalisation. This simple but fundamental statement is briefly illustrated in the following Fig. 1.

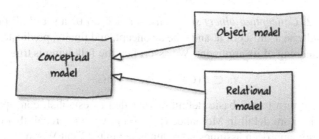

Fig. 1. Conceptual, Relational and Object models.

This basic idea (presumption, conjecture) can be defined more formally as follows[1]:
CONJECTURE 1. *On inheritance. –* Let *CM, RM* and *OM* be the *Conceptual, Relational, and Object Models,* respectively. We assert that the following is true:

$$(RM \subseteq CM) \wedge (OM \subseteq CM) \wedge (RM \not\subseteq OM) \wedge (OM \not\subseteq RM) \qquad (1)$$

---

[1] The formalization is based on intensional sortal modal logics (i.e., intensional modal logics with quantification restricted by sortal) with minimum additions to it [11].

In [3], other assumptions, definitions and lemmas needed to build our approach to conceptual normalisation and conceptual normal forms are defined. These are the following statements, which are justified and defined in more detail in this article.

CONJECTURE 2. *About identity.* – Let *RW* be the *Real World*; *x* and *y* are objects. Next, let the predicate *id* denote identity. We assert that the following is true:

$$\forall(x \in RW)\square\exists id(x) \tag{2}$$

$$(\forall(x \in RW) \wedge \forall(y \in RW)) \to (id(x) = id(y) \to x \equiv y) \tag{3}$$

DEFINITION 1.

A property is a particular characteristic of an object having a value $\qquad$ (4)

∎

LEMMA 1. *Of property uniqueness.* – Let *O* be an object, *p* and *q* be properties of it, and the predicate *in* denotes a set of all properties of that object, and the predicate *cm* denotes a conceptual meaning of that. We assert that the following is true:

$$(\forall(p \in in(O)) \wedge \forall(q \in in(O))) \to (cm(p) = cm(q) \to p \equiv q) \tag{5}$$

THEOREM 1. *Conceptual property atomicity.* – Let *P(O)* be a set of all properties of an object *O*, *p* be a property of it, *c* be a concept, and finally, predicate *cm* denotes a conceptual meaning of its argument. We assert that the following is true:

$$\forall p \in P(O) \to \neg\exists c \subseteq cm(p) \tag{6}$$

THEOREM 2. *Conceptual object simplicity.* – Let *P(O)* be a set of all properties of an object *O*, and *s* be a subset of it, and *c* be a concept, and finally, predicate *cm* denotes a conceptual meaning of its argument. We assert that the following is true:

$$\forall s \subset P(O) \to \neg\exists c = cm(s) \tag{7}$$

We will now turn to the basic definitions needed to establish conceptual normal forms. Again, in more detail in Molhanec ([3]). First, we must recall that our conceptual normalisation approach assumes no redundancy in the Real World. All subsequent considerations of the Author used in this article are based on a fundamental assumption formally formulated as follows:

AXIOM 1. *About non-redundancy.*

There is no redundancy in Real World. $\qquad$ (8)

∎

Redundancy can be informally defined as the absence of identical objects (concepts) in a system. Formal definitions of redundancy and non-redundancy follow.

DEFINITION 2. R*edundant system.* – Let *S* be a system, *x* and *y* be concepts of it, and *cm* be a predicate denoting the conceptual meaning of its argument. We define a predicate *RS* denoting redundant system formally as:

$$RS(S) \stackrel{\text{def}}{=} \square\exists x, y \in S, cm(x) = cm(y) \tag{9}$$

DEFINITION 3. *Non-redundant system.* – Let S be a system, x and y be concepts of it, and cm be a predicate denoting the conceptual meaning of its argument. We define a predicate *NRS* denoting a non-redundant system formally as:

$$NRS(S) \overset{\text{def}}{=} \Box \forall x, y \in S, cm(x) \neq cm(y) \tag{10}$$

We can, therefore, now go a step further and present here the definitions of the conceptual normal forms, which are understood as the rules of non-redundancy already introduced above. We will start this part in detail [Molhanec, 2019] with informal definitions based on the previously presented statements.

DEFINITIONS 4. *Conceptual Normal Forms:*   (11)

- **0CNF**: *There is no redundancy in the Real World.*
- **1CNF**: *A set of object properties is unique in relation to it.*
- **2CNF**: *An object property is not dividable; in other words, the object property is atomic. If we need to work with its part, this part becomes an object of its own, often abstract, with its own properties.*
- **3CNF**: *If we need to work with a group of object properties as if it was one concept, the group becomes an object of its own, often abstract, with its own properties.*

Detailed formal definitions of these informal definitions are in Molhanec [3].

3.2   Relational Normal Forms (RNFs)

The term normalisation, commonly used in the theory of relational databases, was created to remove data redundancy and errors that arise from this. Thus, data normalisation is done, not because someone has defined its forms but for reasons for removing redundancy and errors that may occur when working with such a database. Data redundancy as a source of errors is harmful, and it does not matter whether we are working with a relational or an object database.

The concept of relational normal forms was designed by E. F. Codd [5–7]. Let us briefly summarise their content.

First Relational Normal Form (1RNF)
The problem with 1RNF lies in the fact that this is not the only definition, but at least there are three different definitions where each defines a different rule. They are usually defined as follows.

- **1RNFa**—Each table has a primary key, i.e., a minimum set of attributes to identify the record uniquely. In the Real World, we can only identify natural objects, represented by rows in a data table, using the apparent attributes that the objects contain. Furthermore, this means that different objects must differ in some attributes with a different value for each object. We then call these attributes the Primary Key, usually a minimum set of such attributes. Objects that satisfy this condition are also non-redundant and consistent with our 0CNF presented here.

PROPOSITION 1.

The necessity for the existence of a Primary Key (unique identifier) directly follows from our 0CNF presented here, which, speaking of the necessity of non-redundancy, expresses the same thing differently (12)

- 1RNFb—It is necessary to eliminate the recurring attrib-ute groups with the same meaning by setting them up in a particular table. A repeated set of attributes means that such attributes have the same conceptual meaning within an object. However, this follows from our 1CNF, which says that every attribute of an object is unique.

PROPOSITION 2.

A repeated set of attributes, so 1RNFb, follows from 1CNF presented here, which says that every attribute of an object is unique for it, which is the same thing (13)

- **1RNFc**—Each attribute must contain one value, not a set of values (atomicity).

PROPOSITION 3.

Atomicity, so 1RFN, is a direct consequence of the 2CNF presented here, which defines precisely the same. No further proof is needed. (14)

Second Relational Normal Form (2RNF)

The second relational normal form is usually defined as follows.

- The database must meet all the first normal form requirements.
- All non-key attributes (i.e., attributes not part of the primary Key) depend on the whole Primary Key rather than just a part of it.

In other words, 2RNF requires that each non-key attribute in a table is entirely dependent on the primary Key. Moreover, this means that any attribute that depends on only part of the primary Key must be moved to a separate table to ensure that each attribute in a table depends only on the primary Key. Let us say we have a table called "Sales" with the following attributes:

Order ID (primary Key)

Product ID (primary Key)

Product Name

Product Category

Quantity Sold

Unit Price

In this example, the primary Key comprises two attributes: *Order ID* and *Product ID*. However, the Product Name attribute depends only on the Product ID and does not depend on the entire Primary Key. Furthermore, this violates the 2NF requirement that all non-key attributes must depend on the entire Primary Key. The same also applies to the *Product Category* attribute. The explanation is that *Product ID*, *Product Name* and *Product Category* together have their meaning. They are Real-World separate objects and therefore have to be removed from the existing table into a separate table. Nevertheless, this is what the proposed 3CNF is talking about here.

PROPOSITION 4.
We are convinced that 2RNF is talking about the same as the 3CNF presented here because both normal forms talk about extracting a group of attributes with their own meaning.   (15)

Third Relational Normal Form (3RNF)
The third relational normal form is the most complicated of these three normal forms and is usually defined as follows.

- The database must meet all the requirements of the second normal form.
- Any field that depends on the primary Key through another field (i.e., transitive dependency) moves to a separate table.

Perhaps a better 3RNF definition is as follows: No non-key attribute is transitively dependent on the table key. This expression means that any non-key attribute is not dependent on the table key through another non-key attribute. For example, let us assume a table with the attributes:

Person (Primary Key)

Room

Phone

The Phone is dependent on the attribute *Room*, and the attribute *Room* is dependent on the attribute *Person*, which is also the key attribute of table *Person*. In this case, creating an extra table *Room* with two attributes: a *Primary Key* attribute *Room* and a non-key attribute *Phone* is necessary. Furthermore, we must insert a *Foreign Key* attribute *Room* into the *Person* table.

The 3RNF, like the 2RNF, can be derived from the 3CNF presented here. The reason is the same. The interdependent attributes *Room* and *Phone* represent independent objects of the *Real-World* and, therefore, must be placed in a separate table according to 3CNF.

PROPOSITION 5.
We are convinced that 3RNF is talking about the same as the 3CNF presented here because both normal forms basically extract a group of attributes that have their own meaning   (16)

It may surprise some that 2RNF and 3RNF are derivable from one 3CNF. However, this is not surprising; if we leave the RNF language and go to the CNF language, we see that in both cases it is an exclusion of a group of attributes that claim their own existence. The only difference is that in the case of 2RNF, the *Primary Key* of the extracted object participates in the *Primary Key* of the original object, and this is not the case with 3RNF.

PROPOSITION 6.
We are convinced that 2RNF and 3RNF are fundamentally identical if we explain them in a language based on the principles of CNF because both normal forms are talking about extracting a group of attributes that have their own meaning   (17)

4   Results

Based on the previous propositions, the Author claims that the well-known RNF can be derived from the CNF proposed here.

Briefly summarized. The basis for this claim comes from the fact that 1RNF deals with the atomicity of data attributes, the prohibition of multi-attributes and the necessity of primary key existence. The atomicity issue relates to the herein proposed 2CNF, the prohibition of multi-attributes results from 1CNF and the issue of the necessity of the primary key existence relates to principal 0CNF.

Further, the Author suggests that both 2RNF and 3RNF follow from the above-suggested 3CNF. The evidence is based on the consideration that the existence of transitive dependency between attributes in the data table at the level of the relational data paradigm is simply an implication of the incorrect recognition of conceptual objects and their relationships at a higher level of comprehensibility.

Here we must recall a fact that is perhaps not so obvious. The unique identity of an object is given not only by the values stored in its attributes (Primary Key) but also by the relationships in which it exists. It follows that Foreign Keys can also be part of the Primary Key.

Finally, it is worth noting that the concept of Foreign Keys in relational database systems represents only a programmer's implementation of relationships between conceptual objects. Thus, the misrecognition of the proper objects at the conceptual level leads to a transitive dependency between attributes at the relational level.

Perhaps now one heretical remark, resulting from the Author's experience as a conceptual analyst. The theory of database normalisation and its three normal forms shows how to normalise a poorly designed database (database schema), i.e., a set of their tables and their attributes. However, according to the Author's opinion, a correctly performed analysis at the conceptual level practically automatically leads to a good scheme directly from its principle. It is even more unfortunate that students strongly underestimate the analysis stage and devote their interest far more to technical matters than thinking about concepts.

Finally, the connections between all normal forms are shown in Fig. 2 and Table 1.

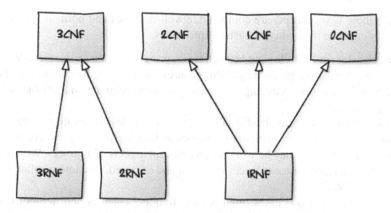

Fig. 2. Connectedness between CNFs and RNFs

Table 1. The connection between CNF and RNF

CNF	RNF	Note
0	1	non-redundancy
1	1	uniqueness
2	1	atomicity
3	2 + 3	non-transitivity

5 Conclusion and Future Works

In this contribution, the Author deals with the connections between conceptual and relational normalisation. A proper understanding of these connections brings practical benefits. Classic relational normalisation deals primarily with database keys and their values. However, we are primarily concerned with the meaning of classes, objects, and properties on a conceptual level. This approach allows us to think about the whole problem at a higher level of abstraction. Also, it allows us to understand the problem better and create the correct model. The result can be a correct relational model because we start from a higher abstraction of reality.

Better theory for database normalization can certainly improve agile business process design. Database normalization is the process of organizing data in a database to reduce redundancy and improve data integrity. By applying normalization techniques, data is structured in a way that minimizes duplication and ensures that each piece of information is stored in one place, leading to a more efficient and reliable database design [12–14].

Agile business process design, on the other hand, is an approach that focuses on flexibility, adaptability, and iterative development to meet the changing needs of the business. It emphasizes collaboration, continuous improvement, and rapid response to customer feedback.

When these two concepts are combined, a well-designed and normalized database can greatly enhance the agility of business processes.

- Data consistency: By following normalization principles, data is organized in a consistent manner across the database. This ensures that there are no conflicting or contradictory information, reducing errors and providing accurate and reliable data for agile processes.
- Data integration: A normalized database enables seamless integration of data from various sources. This is particularly important in agile processes where different teams or stakeholders may be working on different aspects of a project. With a well-structured database, data can be easily shared and accessed, promoting collaboration and efficiency.
- Adaptability: Agile processes often require frequent changes and iterations. With a normalized database, making changes to the structure or design becomes easier and less prone to errors. This allows businesses to quickly adapt their data models to accommodate evolving requirements, supporting the iterative nature of agile processes.
- Scalability: As businesses grow, the amount of data they handle also increases. A properly normalized database can handle scalability more effectively by minimizing redundancy and optimizing storage. This ensures that the database can accommodate the expanding data needs of an agile business without sacrificing performance or compromising data integrity.
- Performance optimization: Database normalization helps in reducing data duplication, which in turn improves query performance. In an agile environment where rapid response times are crucial, an optimized database design can significantly enhance the speed and efficiency of data retrieval and manipulation operations.

By leveraging a better theory for database normalization, businesses can establish a strong foundation for their data management practices. This, in turn, positively impacts the design and execution of agile business processes, facilitating flexibility, collaboration, and responsiveness to changing requirements and market conditions.

Surprisingly, this fundamental topic, i.e., the conceptual foundations of relational normalization, is not widely discussed by the professional public. Database designers are at their low relational level, seeing the system only as a set of tables linked by foreign keys and not seeing the database as a conceptual model of the real World. However, this low level of vision brings, in the Author's opinion, shortcomings in the design of the database, which are manifested in various ways, for example, redundancy, a non-correct structure of attributes, and a wrong schema of the database.

References

1. Molhanec, M.: Towards the conceptual normalisation. In: Proceedings of the 6th International Workshop on Enterprise & Organizational Modeling and Simulationm pp. 133–141. CEUR-WS. org (2010)
2. Molhanec, M.: Conceptual normalisation formalised. In: Workshop on Enterprise and Organizational Modeling and Simulation, pp. 159–172. Springer (2011)

3. Molhanec, M.: Conceptual normalisation in software engineering. In: Pergl, R., Babkin, E., Lock, R., Malyzhenkov, P., Merunka, V. (eds.) EOMAS 2019. LNBIP, vol. 366, pp. 18–28. Springer, Cham (2019). https://doi.org/10.1007/978-3-030-35646-0_2

4. Molhanec, M.: Some reasoning behind conceptual normalisation. In: Pokorny, J., et al. (eds.) Information Systems Development, pp. 517–525. Springer, New York (2011). https://doi.org/10.1007/978-1-4419-9790-6_41

5. Codd, E.F.: A relational model of data for large shared data banks. Commun. ACM. **13**, 377–387 (1970)

6. Codd, E.F.: Further normalization of the data base relational model. Data Base Syst. 33–64 (1972)

7. Codd, E. F.: Recent Investigations into Relational Data Base Systems

8. Chen, P.P.-S.: The entity-relationship model—toward a unified view of data. ACM Trans. Database Syst. TODS. **1**, 9–36 (1976)

9. Benci, E., Bodart, F., Bogaert, H., Cabanes, A.: Concepts for the design of a conceptual schema. In: IFIP Working Conference on Modelling in Data Base Management Systems, pp. 181–200 (1976)

10. Halpin, T.A.: What is an elementary fact? In: Proceedings of First NIAM-ISDM Conference on Utrecht (1993)

11. Guizzardi, G., Wagner, G., Guarino, N., van Sinderen, M.: An ontologically well-founded profile for UML conceptual models. In: Persson, A., Stirna, J. (eds.) Advanced Information Systems Engineering, pp. 112–126. Springer, Berlin Heidelberg (2004). https://doi.org/10.1007/978-3-540-25975-6_10

12. Connolly, T., Begg, C.: Database Systems: A Practical Approach to Design, Implementation, and Management. Pearson, Boston (2014)

13. Ambler, S.: Agile Database Techniques: Effective Strategies for the Agile Software Developer. Wiley, Indianapolis, IN (2003)

14. Hughes, R.: Agile Data Warehousing Project Management: Business Intelligence Systems Using Scrum. Morgan Kaufmann, Waltham, MA (2012)

Application of an Agent-Based Simulation for a Definition of a Trade-Off Retail Price Promotion Strategy

Boris Ulitin$^{(\boxtimes)}$ (iD), Eduard Babkin (iD), Tatiana Babkina (iD), Igor Ulitin (iD), and Marina Zubova

HSE University, Moscow, Russia
{bulitin,eababkin,tbabkina,iulitin}@hse.ru

Abstract. A good pricing strategy is a key aspect of the company's product success. In the context of business agility, the company's ability to quickly respond to changes in purchasing power and demand allows not only to take a leading position in the market, but also guarantee its development for years to come. However, the interactions between companies and customers add complexity to companies pricing decisions. On the other hand, there are agent-based approach, which can help to analyze pricing strategy, focusing on the interactions between companies and customers. Customer buying decisions are influenced by several customer preferences factors, while product prices depend on the company's promotion strategy. The promotion is applied based on the frequency and depth of the price cut. The results show that the limited rationality and interactions of each agent drive the unique behavior of the system and affect companies profit and market share according to its pricing strategy.

Keywords: competition model · business agility · multi-agent modelling · customer behavior model

1 Introduction

Agent-based models (ABMs) have great prospects for research in socio-economic systems. One of the most interesting areas of work in the framework of multi-agent modeling is the study of competition between different agents [2]. Analytical models make it possible to obtain illustrative results, but one has to pay for clarity by introducing additional assumptions into the model, such as: an infinite population size, limiting the number of possible behavior strategies, ignoring the spatial structure of the population [4].

In the context of business agility, ABMs makes it possible to evaluate the potential effects of managerial decisions on company performance over any time horizon [12]. This is especially important in the context of determining the optimal strategy for the development of the company, which depends on such factors as the cost of the goods/services provided, their quality, as well as the availability and practice of using marketing programs. At the same time, dependence is also observed between the factors:

© The Author(s), under exclusive license to Springer Nature Switzerland AG 2023
E. Babkin et al. (Eds.): MOBA 2023, LNBIP 488, pp. 42–52, 2023.
https://doi.org/10.1007/978-3-031-45010-5_4

the cost of services is directly determined by the quality of goods/services and the costs of marketing programs, as well as the competitive environment for the functioning of the company [13]. And in this sense, the search for the optimal strategy for the development of the task becomes a non-trivial task, since the competitive environment has a high degree of unpredictability.

A separate agent (firm) is usually described in competition models as follows [3]: the agent's sensory system provides perception of the external world from the field of view of the agent and supplies the agent with information about his inner state. The agent is oriented in space. The agent has the "forward" direction relative to which its field of vision is oriented, and the actions they take are defined. The agent's field of view consists of 4 cells: one the cell in which the agent is located, as well as the cells located in front of the agent, on the right and to the left of the agent. In its field of view, the agent can see other agents and interact with them. Each firm is capable of running a set of certain actions (programs) to improve its performance [4].

As for the agent-client, it usually is modeled as a randomly-moving agent that can either transact with a company if certain conditions are met, or it can ɯavoid transaction in case if conditions are not met. The client may incorporate different preference characteristics that aim to model its probability to interact with certain agents firms [5].

However, the question of researching the company's development strategy to attract the maximum number of customers remains the most relevant. Taking into account the long-term development strategy, the issue of combining development tools for the company to reach the peak of its development and agility remains controversial. For example, in [6] it is noted that the constant use of the same tools leads to a decrease in their effectiveness, and even has a negative effect on the development of the company.

On the other hand, the simultaneous use of various instruments is expensive and bears certain risks on the financial performance of the company. An example of such a negative use of market tools is the experience of Friends Reunited, which tried to expand the volume of promotions without increasing production capacity, as a result, faced with server crashes and the loss of half of the customers [5].

One strategic decision for company in terms of this task is pricing: where a firm sets the value in the exchange of goods and services. An appropriate pricing strategy can increase sales and win market share for a company because price is an essential source of information for customers when making purchase decisions [9]. However, many factors must be considered when making pricing decisions, including understanding consumer behavior and the competition between companies [5].

Consumer behavior is influenced by consumer preference, which drives customer actions in choosing a company and determining the buying quantity [4]. Consumer preferences can be defined as the buying priorities of consumers where each consumer has a different preference. Preferences can be induced by many factors, including: socio-demographic factors, such as age and income; personality, including sensitivity to price, distance, and quality; and factors related to interaction – the exchange of information with the company [7]. In addition to customer preferences, it is also necessary to pay attention to reference prices that affect customer reactions. The reference price is the standard value of the product to the customer that influences their decision to buy [8].

There are many approaches in the literature to address the issue of pricing strategies. Some of them take into account the context of business agility. For example, [14] contains an example of how a company's sustainability reports are included in a pricing strategy. Several other studies address multi-channel pricing strategies using a mathematical approach that considers supplier relationships, inter-channel competition, and customer behavior [3, 5, 7] demonstrates how company can make product choice decisions and determine pricing policies by considering heterogeneous customer demand based on different customer values. Money-back guarantees (MBGs), which allow customers to return products that do not meet their expectations, are widely used in the retail industry [9]. Another model designed a two-stage dynamic pricing strategy when sellers face strategic consumers in the presence of a reference price effect [8]: customers with different time-sensitivities need different approaches and the right pricing strategy to address this problem. However, none of these studies allow for modelling the interactions between consumers and companies, an important part of the decision-making process in the trade of a product or service.

Thus, we will try to combine in this study the experience of several companies, both successful and unsuccessful, in order to model the trade-off pricing strategy for the development of the company. In the Sect. 2 we summarize the possible actions the company can take to attract new customers and develop itself and the details of the developed multi-agent model. Section 3 demonstrates the analysis of the behavior of the model with different basic parameters. Section 4 presents the simulation results and conclusions from the work, continuing in the Conclusion.

The research is supported by grant of the Russian Science Foundation (project № 23–21-00112 "Models and methods to support sustainable development of socio-technical systems in digital transformation under crisis conditions").

2 Agent-Based Model Description

Based on the idea that the main source of income and functioning of the company is to attract customers, in the developed model, we extend the modelling framework from [10], which addresses the following elements of a conceptual model: the model content, inputs or experimental factors, outputs or responses, and assumptions and simplifications of the model. The model content incorporates the main features of the agent-based modelling approach, which describe the model's scope and level of detail.

The model consists of agents, environment, interactions, and rules of behavior. There are 2 types of agents in our model: firms and clients.

To identify the characteristics of each agent types, we analyze existing psychological and economic research in the field of market relations: consumer price reference theory for the gain and loss aspect, consumer behavior theory, and price promotion theory. In accordance with the confirmed Croom et al. hypotheses [7], the essential characteristics taken into account by the buyer in the process of making a purchase decision are the amount of free cash and the expected level of service (goods quality). In addition, the presence of a positive experience of interaction with the company has an impact [1]. Finally, the customers decision to shop is influenced by the distance model as well as price. Firms are located relatively close to each other, while customers are located randomly and dynamically in the environment.

On the part of the company, the following characteristics can be determined: the price of a good (or a service), the quality of the services provided, the size of the discount for various categories of customers (in the case of the model being created, we will consider one averaged parameter not to complicate the model), the loyalty of the company's customers. By loyalty, we understand, as in the case of a client, the number of successful interactions between a company and a client. Most often, 3 categories of customer loyalty are distinguished [7]: random customer (who made 1 purchase), potentially loyal (made a repeat purchase) and loyal (made more than 2 purchases).

Agent-firms can be set to have either homogenous or heterogeneous behavior in making pricing decisions. The firm's pricing decisions are related to price promotion, defined by the frequency and level of price reduction. The pricing method applies a cost-plus strategy, while the price promotion reduces the target profit. The promotion strategy is delineated into three levels: high-shallow, moderate and low-deep [6]. The high-shallow strategy represents a high frequency, shallow price cut, where the price reduction is around 20% with 40% of occurrences. The moderate strategy reflects a moderate frequency and level of price cut, which provides a price reduction of about 40% in 20% of occurrences. The low-deep strategy consists of a low frequency, deep price cut, with a price reduction of about 80% in 10% of occurrences. When companies are set to be homogenous, they both adopt a similar price promotion strategy; when they are set to be heterogeneous, the companies apply different pricing strategies.

Based on the prerequisites above, **Client** is modeled with the following **properties**: price, distance, gain and loss tolerance, and budget. Each consumer possesses a different weight for each type of preference, so the consumers are set to be heterogeneous. For example, some consumer agents can be highly sensitive to price, while others have different features. Consumers also have various budgets that follow a normal distribution, so that each consumer has a diverse budget. This rule gives each consumer a different level of demand, i.e. each consumer can generate a different number of items to buy.

The "client" agent is aimed to have few characteristics and possibilities in the model proposed, as we focus mainly on firms and their behavior. Some customer-related logic is incorporated into firms to make it more representative on the level of the firm.

The "firm" agent is modeled with the following characteristics:

- *product-price* (indicates the base price of the product for the client);
- *service-level* (indicates the level of service the firm is able to provide for the clients);
- *n-success/n-refused* (two additional parameters to indicate the number of successful and unsuccessful transactions of each firm with each client);
- *first-category/second-category/third-category* (parameters to store information about what customers buy only one, twice, and more than twice times in each firm);
- *loyalty-discount* (the number (percent) to apply as discount to the product-price for loyal customers);
- *n-loyal-success* (indicates the number of transactions that implied loyal customers and usage of discount);

The interactions between agents are illustrated as follows. The consumer agents select a company that fits their preference. For instance, if a consumer agent is more sensitive to price than company distance, then it needs to consider the gap between the desired price and the lowest price offered by the company. If the gap is still within its loss tolerance, the consumer will select the company that provides a lower price. Otherwise, the consumer will not decide to buy from any of the companies. When the consumer decides to buy from one of the two companies, the next decision determines the number of items to buy, depending on the budget of the consumer. The main customer-firm interaction logic is written under the transaction function (Fig. 1) that aims to check if a certain client is able to buy a specific product of the specific company.

```
to make-transaction
  ask customers-on companies [
    set color random-range 20 30
    let customer-who who
    let customer-offer constant-budget
    let customer-preference-service-level preference-service-level

    ask companies-here [
      ifelse member? customer-who third-category
      and customer-offer >= ( product-price - ( product-price * loyality-discount ) )
      [ set n-success n-success + 1
        set n-loyal-success n-loyal-success + 1 ]
      [
      ifelse customer-offer >= product-price
      and customer-preference-service-level <= service-level
      [ set n-success n-success + 1
        ifelse not member? customer-who first-category
        [set first-category lput customer-who first-category ]
        [ ifelse not member? customer-who second-category
          [ set second-category lput customer-who second-category ]
          [ if not member? customer-who third-category
            [ set third-category lput customer-who third-category ]
          ]
        ]
      ]
      [ set n-refused n-refused + 1 ]
      ]
    ]
  ]
end
```

Fig. 1. The listing of the function defining the behavior of the Clients

The company behavior is presented as the pricing strategy used and the following characteristics can be determined: the price of a good (or a service), the quality of the services provided, the size of the discount for various categories of customers (in the case of the model being created, we will consider one averaged parameter not to complicate the model), the loyalty of the company's customers. Most often, 3 categories of customer loyalty are distinguished [7]: random customer (who made 1 purchase), potentially loyal (made a repeat purchase) and loyal (made more than 2 purchases). These characteristics are internal to the company and can be managed, bringing the company closer to the context of agility. However, in this case, the flexibility itself is provided not by the characteristics, but by the behavior model of the agents of the model. The promotion strategy is set to be the key input or experimental factor of the model that affects the consumer's buying behavior. In what follows, the emergent outcome of the simulation is measured by three indicators: company profit, total sales, and market share.

At the start of the program, the number of companies is created in the world. This number is specified by the user in the interface. Each company has different size, unique color, "house" shape, and the set of parameters: product price (ranges are specified by user in the interface), service level (can be either randomized or set to the first service level by user in the interface), n-success/n-refused parameters (set to 0 at the start), first-second-third categories of the customers (set to 0 at the start), and finally the number of discount (set to 0 at the start), and the number of transactions with loyal clients (as well 0).

Customer is initialized with a random budget from the specified by the user range in the user interface. And then, each customer is initialized with the random level of service preference. The number of customers can be set in the user interface as well.

Each turn customers are randomly moving in the world and start a transaction with companies around. Additionally, during this function we check for every 2000 ticks to allow companies to start their programs. There is another condition for stopping the model after 50000 ticks as well. This option is available for users in the interface, so the model can be run either in infinite mode or with the restriction with 50000 ticks only.

The results show that when both retailers have a homogeneous competitive behavior, the emergent outcomes are in accordance with Hotelling's law. The second validation process against the model is seen from the consumer behavior in choosing companies. From the customer model, it can be seen that customers are making decisions according to their respective preferences, in accordance with real conditions [7]. The final validation is that the company's behavior in determining the price promotion has illustrated the transition between frequency and price cut [8].

In what follows we demonstrates the preliminary results of the model, covering a small number of experiments analyzing the effect of price promotion strategy on retailers. Our model supports several user interactions and presetting scenarios. The user can set (Fig. 2) the number of clients and firms to be in the model world. This is the reason why we call this model n-based. The user can set upper and lower bounds of the client's budget and product price. These numbers will be used as ranges for random generation while creating agents. The user can specify the model running mode: infinite or strict with 50000 ticks (it is usually enough for the model performance and results getting). The user can manipulate starting company service-level as well. In our case, the number of competing companies is limited to 10.

According to the idea, that we compare 3 possible pricing strategies in pairs, we are dealing with 6 possible cases:

- *Homogeneous cases:*

  - all companies apply the high-shallow strategy;
  - all companies adopt a moderate strategy;
  - all companies follow the low-deep strategy;

- *Heterogenies cases:*

  - companies use a moderate/the high-shallow strategies in some proportion;
  - companies apply a moderate/the low-deep strategies in some proportion;

- companies apply the high-shallow/the low-deep strategies in some proportion.

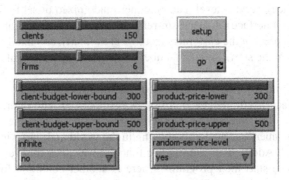

Fig. 2. User controllers for the agents' parameters

The results of replicated data from the simulation results of 100 replications for *Homogeneous cases* indicates (according to Welch's t-test with a confidence level of 95%) that the difference in average profit between the companies is insignificant. A similar emergent pattern also applies to the total sales. The reason for this small difference in profit and sales between retailers could be because of the identical price promotion strategy used by the retailers. It is coherent with [11], that if N retailers have the same price, promotion, product, and adjacent location, the benefits received by the N do not have a significant difference. It is also proved by comparing profit summary for companies in these scenarios (Table 1). This means that in the case when companies use an identical pricing strategy, the final results of the companies turn out to be close () and only their value depends on the chosen strategy.

Table 1. Profit summary for Homogeneous cases

Profit	High-shallow	Moderate	Low-deep
Mean	100 402	101 003	100 001
Median	99 730	100 681	99 041
Minimum	99 921	100 518	98 932
Maximum	100 860	101 870	100 800

At the same time, Welch's t-test for *Heterogenies cases* showed a significant difference in the average profit received by companies.

Comparing moderate strategy vs. high-shallow strategy, we see, that in the beginning of the simulation each strategy alternated in dominating profit and sales during the simulation run. However, when the simulation length extended to be more than 500 ticks, the moderate strategy was the dominant strategy in terms of profit and total sales (Fig. 3).

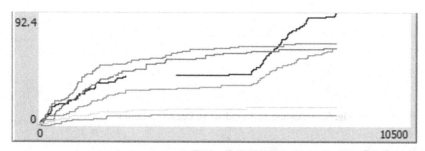

Fig. 3. Moderate vs. high-shallow strategies scenarios results

Comparing a high-shallow vs. low-deep strategies, we can see that a high-shallow strategy leads to higher profits and sales than a low-deep strategy (Fig. 4). Summarizing profits for companies with the same strategies and comparing them, it can be seen that companies with a high-shallow strategy reached its highest profit in contrast to companies that used a low-deep strategy (Table 2).

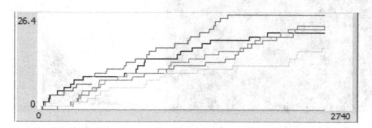

Fig. 4. High-shallow vs. low-deep strategies scenarios results

Table 2. Profit summary for High-shallow vs. low-deep strategies scenarios

Profit	High-shallow	low-deep
Mean	110 432	56 092
Median	109 730	55 118
Minimum	108 921	55 003
Maximum	110 860	56 990

Finally, for moderate vs. low-deep strategies no strategy consistently dominated in terms of profit and sales during the simulation run (Fig. 5).

By repeating the results with different strategies, we can find the following generalized results (Fig. 6). Only in case of competing High-shallow vs. low-deep strategies there is a significant difference in profit obtained by High-shallow strategies adepts.

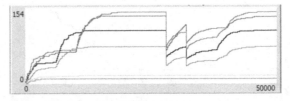

Fig. 5. Moderate vs. low-deep strategies scenarios results

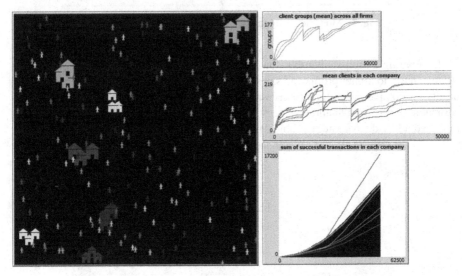

Fig. 6. Model behavior with the same service-level for all companies

The type of price promotion strategy had an influence on consumer demand, particularly in the quantity of goods purchased. When neither company applied any promotion, the total consumer demand was about 22 thousand units. The demand increased when the price promotion strategies were applied. The scenarios, described above, generated demand for about 24–26-26–26-27–27 thousand units respectively. In this context, only two last scenarios resulted in higher demand generation.

3 Agent-Based Model Analysis

Depending on the parameters we enter in the user interface, we can get different results of model running. There are several interesting trends and scenarios. First of all, each base run with preset parameters shows us base competition of the companies and during that competition some of the companies take a lead by applying more effective strategies, while other companies remain on the same level, constantly struggling between each other and trying to adjust product pricing.

Furthermore, in case of using different strategies we see different results for demand generation: only two last scenarios resulted in higher demand generation. These outcomes are a result of the bounded-rationality of the agents in the model. The consumer agents updated their behavior over time, but the companies did not have any information about the future actions of the consumers. The consumers also could not predict when the companies would apply a promotion and so refreshed their decisions in each time unit of the simulation. Furthermore, the companies did not have enough information about the pricing decisions made by their competitor, or when the competitor would apply its own promotion strategy.

On the other hand, different manipulations with product pricing and customer budget may lead to interesting results too. If we set the highest product pricing ranges possible, we get the longest competition between companies during the whole run. Only up to the middle-end of the run some companies are able to take a distinct lead in the market. If we start with the same service-level for all companies, we will get the longest companies development time and sometimes there is not enough time for the model to start showing companies development in the 50000 ticks timeframe. That is, we recommend a random service-level preset for the world, as it models a more real-life situation on the market.

It is important to pay attention to the fact that the initial price of the goods does not have such a big effect as the level of quality. In most experiments, at the end of the model (or from a certain point, about 49,000 ticks from the start), companies with the highest price of the product and low customer coverage or companies with a lower price and maximum customer coverage showed similar revenue results.

4 Conclusion

Thus, in this paper, a multi-agent model of competition of various companies in the market was considered. The model can provide different scenarios on the same parameters presets, but overall those scenarios will follow the same trend. Some companies lead the market by expanding their business and upgrading service-level, while other companies struggle with each other in the price wars.

Based on the results of the experiments, we argue, that not all price promotion strategies are effective under most circumstances. The high-shallow strategy is found to be the only approach that has a significant result in improving retailer profits, sales, and market share. However, this situation only applies when the other retailer adopts a low-deep strategy. This emergent behavior is due to the bounded-rationality of the agents.

These results are somewhat different from existing views on the strategy of companies based on the principle of price fairness in terms of product quality [7, 8]. According to the data obtained, the price of the goods has an impact only at the initial moment of the company's development, ultimately not significantly affecting the results of the company's work in terms of the number of attracted customers and profits.

Our agent-based model provides a new way to understand the impact of pricing strategies on companies, while consolidating various features of consumers. However, the heterogeneous agents make it difficult for the analysis to trace which customer preferences are sensitive to each of these price promotion strategies. Another aspect to be considered for future research is the limited number of simulated retailers. More competing retailers may lead to different emergent results.

Compared to existing pricing models [5, 8, 9], our model allows experts to evaluate the effectiveness of a company's ideas and principles of agility in the context of its interaction with customers. The results of experiments show that in the case when companies use an identical pricing strategy, agility tools do not have a significant effect on the resulting profit of the company and its market share. However, in the case of a heterogeneous market environment, the mechanisms of flexibility and adaptability of the company to demand and purchasing power become decisive, as they allow the company to use the best pricing strategy and achieve a leading position in the market.

References

1. Gupta, et al.: Information technology and profitability: evidence from Indian banking sector. Inter. J. Emerging Markets **13**(5), 1070–1087 (2018)
2. Karthikvel, S., Samydoss, C.: Organizational contention and confrontation to sustainable development: a socio-economic prospective. Shodh Sanchar Bull. **10**(38), 69–73 (2020)
3. Martins, H.C.: Competition and ESG practices in emerging markets: evidence from a difference-in-differences model. Finance Res. Lett. 46A (2022)
4. Pennerstorfer, D., Yontcheva, B.: Local market definition in competition analysis: an application to entry models. Econ. Lett. **198** (2021)
5. Richards, T.J., Hamilton, S.F., Yonezawa, K.: Retail market power in a shopping basket model of supermarket competition. J. Retailing **94**(3), 328–342 (2018)
6. Sun, S., Wang, W.: Analysis on the market evolution of new energy vehicle based on population competition model. Trans. Res. Part D: Trans. Environ. **65**, 36–50 (2018)
7. Croom, S., Fritzon, K., Brooks, N.: Personality differences and buyer-supplier relationships: psychopathy in executives, gender differences and implications for future research. J. Purchasing Supply Manag. **27**(4) (2021)
8. DeCarlo, T.E., Hansen, J.D.: Examining buyers' negative word-of-mouth intentions following suspected salesperson transgressions. Industrial Market. Manag. **102**, 35–44 (2022)
9. Vrânceanu, D.M., Ţuclea, C.E., Ţigu, G.: Price search behaviour in digital markets-A perspective from Romania. Manag. Marketing **15**(2), 219–235 (2020)
10. Robinson, S.: Simulation the Practice of Model Development and Use. John Wiley & Sons Ltd., England (2004)
11. Ridley, D.B.: Hotelling's Law. In: The Palgrave Encyclopedia of Strategic Management (2016)
12. Markou, C., Koulinas, G.K., Vavatsikos, A.P.: Project resources scheduling and leveling using multi-attribute decision models: models implementation and case study. Expert Syst. Appli. **77**, 160–169 (2017)
13. Nonaka, I., Kodama, M., Hirose, A., Kohlbacher, F.: Dynamic fractal organizations for promoting knowledge-based transformation – A new paradigm for organizational theory. Eur. Manag. J. **32**(1), 137–146 (2014)
14. Japee, G., Oza, P.: Redefining sustainable development. Psychology **58**(2), 5610–5619 (2021)

Business Process Models and Eye Tracking System for BPMN Evaluation-Usability Study

Josef Pavlicek[1(✉)], Petra Pavlickova[2], Alžběta Pokorná[2], and Matej Brnka[2]

[1] Faculty of Information Technology, CTU, Thákurova 9, Prague 6 160 00, Czech Republic
josef.pavlicek@fit.cvut.cz

[2] Faculty of Economics and Management, Czech University of Life Sciences, Kamýcká 129, Prague 6 165 00, Czech Republic
petra.pavlickova@fit.cvut.cz, {pokornaa,brnka}@pef.czu.cz

Abstract. This paper deals with eye tracking system used for BPMN models usability testing. The research was based on participants running eye tracking tests relating to typical real-life situations by focusing on documenting the processes involved in real-life testing of the below areas. Eye tracking can help us record what catches a user's eye on a visual display. It can give invaluable insight into the process model by BPMN. It has a potential to become an industry standard for designing and developing process models. There has been a perfect start of progress in eye tracking technologies to make participants friendly.

Keywords: BPMN models · BPMN elements · HCI · eye tracking system · Usability study

1 Introduction

Our team has been working for many years on the use of HCI technologies to improve the quality of process models. In the past years, we have shown that there is a dependency between the complexity of an operation (which is defined by a shape with a description) and the effort a user has to spend to understand it. We have shown that the BPMN notation is readable enough for both experts and lay or naive users. Not surprisingly, the decision block (as a node with one input and two outputs) introduces more complexity in understanding its meaning. Of course, this is in terms of the process, not in terms of the semantics of the model. Current technologies to verify this phenomenon can be built on eye cameras.

Eye tracking system is a method that can serve as a valuable tool in HCI. The objective of using eye tracking is to understand a user's point of view or we can say it is a technique whereby the individual's eye movements are measured so that we know where a person is gazing at any given time and the sequence in which their eyes are shifting from one location to another. That helps us to understand visual and information processing that can be provided as an objective source of interface evaluation data which can inform the design of improved interfaces. BPMN is considered as a new path for describing business

E. Babkin et al. (Eds.): MOBA 2023, LNBIP 488, pp. 53–64, 2023.
https://doi.org/10.1007/978-3-031-45010-5_5

process semantics which the notation is easy to comprehend and highly understandable to managing the organization.

The BPMN 1.0 was upgraded by the Business Process Management institute (BPMI), which is now combined with the object Management Group (OMG) and released publicly in May 2004 and adopted as OMG standard in 2006 [1].

The earliest known research according to the acceptance of BPMN was managed in 2006, which is reasonable since the standard was first launched in 2004. BPMN was recently presented as a standard driven by the demand for a graphical notation that accompanies the BPEL4WS standard for practicable business processes.

Three years after the launch of BPMN, an article from 2007 presented a business process modelling game to learn BPMN 1.0 notation. The article reported that the serious game could be a good opportunity to enrich higher education to stimulate scenarios of the real world and to enhance didactics for students that was addressed in 2008 where the authors declared that BPMN is accepted and used among businesspeople and academics [2].

There is a perspective of BPMN acceptance which existed in an article in 2008 [3–5] about BPMN 1.0 was used in groups of several, Well-defined construct clusters but less than 20% of its vocabulary was regularly used and some constructs did not occur in any of the model analyzed [3, 6].

2   Materials and Methods

2.1   BPMN Diagram Elements and Symbols

A business process model and notation diagram for short, is utilized to create simple and easy to read business process model flowcharts, whilst at the same time being able to handle the complexity inheritance to Business Processes.

These two conflicting requirements were to organize the graphical viewpoints of the notation into particularly categories. These bring a small set of notation categories so that the reader can easily acknowledge the basic types of elements. Additional to this, variance and information can be included to support the requirements for complexity without changing the basic look.

There are 5 basic categories of elements are:

- Flow objects
- Data
- Connecting Objects
- Swim lanes
- Artefacts

Flow objects: They are the main elements which represent all the activities or define the behavior of a business process. There are three flow objects:

- Events
- Activities
- Gateways

2.2 Basic BPMN Modelling Elements

Events: An Event is something that occurs during the course of a process or a Choreography. They affect the flow of the model and usually have a **trigger** or an impact (**result**). We will notice that Events are Circles with open centers to permit internal markers to differentiate different triggers or results [7].

There are three types of Events: Start, intermediate, End.

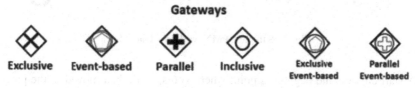

Fig. 1. BPMN Events Symbols

Gateway: A Gateway is utilised to control the divergence and convergence of sequence Flows in a process which means, it will be determined, branching, merging, or joining of path. So, the internal markers will indicate the type of behaviour control. The gateway can be exclusive, parallel or complex.

Fig. 2. BPMN Gateway Symbols and Types of Gateways

Activity: An Activity is a generic term for work that a company performs in the process. it can be atomic or non-atomic (compound). The type of activities contains Sub-Process and Task, that are rounded rectangles.

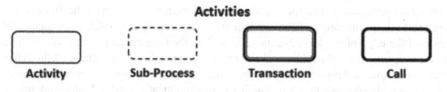

Fig. 3. BPMN Activity Symbols

Sequence Flow: A sequence flow is used to indicate the order of activities that will be performed in a process.

Message Flow: A message Flow is used to indicate the flow of messages between two participants that are prepared to send and receive them.

Association: An Association is an act of connecting or linking information and artefacts with BPMN graphical elements.

Sequence Flow   **Message Flow**

Fig. 4. BPMN Sequence flow   **Fig. 5.** BPMN Message Flow

Association

Fig. 6. BPMN Association Flow

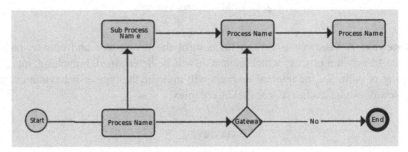

Fig. 7. Sample BPMN workflow Diagram

A start circle is the beginning point where you started, then moved to the process **name**. From this point you have 2 options to continue: Sub process name and Gateway. If there will be no process, then finish the process (**End**).

2.3 Eye Tracking Technology

The use of eye tracking technology was first developed in reading research over 100 years ago. It was started in the 19th century. The historical methods need the wearing of huge contact lenses that covered the cornea (the clear membrane covered the front of the eye) and sclera (the white of the eye which is seen from the outside), with metal coil inserted the edge of the lens, eye movement were then measured by fluctuations in an electromagnetic field when the metal coil moved along with the eyes. These methods had proved invasive, and most modern eye tracking system nowadays utilizes video images of the eye to determine where a person is gazing ("point-of-regard"). Many recognizing features of the eye tracking can be utilized to infer point-of -regard, such as corneal reflections (known as Purkinje image), the iris-sclera boundary, and the apparent pupil shape.

Most modern eye trackers use near-infrared technology along with high-resolution cameras (or other optical sensors) to track gaze direction. It is commonly referred to as Pupil Centre Corneal Reflection (PCCR). The infrared light from an LED inserted in the infrared camera is first going through into the eye to build strong reflections in target eye features to make it effortless to track (an infrared light is utilized to avoid dazzling the user with visible light). The light enters the retina and a big proportion of it is reflected, which makes the pupil show as bright. The corneal reflection is also created by the infrared light, appearing as tiny as you see below.

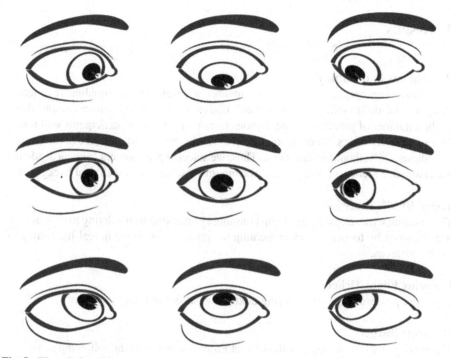

Fig. 8. The relative difference in location of the pupil center and corneal reflection deduction of the gaze direction

2.4   How to Use Eye Tracking

If the guests are connected to eye tracking system, we have an opportunity to say:

- What they look at on the screen or in the real world.
- When attention is set on the certain visual elements.
- How long each fixation lasts for.
- How their center moves from thing on our site page.
- What parts of the interface they miss.
- How they are exploring the length of the page.
- How size and arrangement of things on your current site or on proposed structure influences consideration.

2.5   The Usability Study Research Approach

The research method chosen (eye tracking Usability testing) was qualitative – cognitive walkthrough [9], this method provided information on BPMN eye tracking study via the following:

- From the movement define, which symbols were difficult to understand (Eye tracking heatmap).
- Collection of information from participants after the eye tracking test (primarily for the hypothesis validation).

3 Results

Participants in the Study

Selecting an appropriate number of participants is a key element of a qualitative usability study. We decided to follow Jacob Nilesen's research. While he does not recommend any explicit number of participants, he demonstrates that roughly 5 participants will reveal 75% of usability errors. Since we are interested in the power and influence of the defined hypotheses, 75% should be sufficient. Thus, we selected 5 volunteers from an academic background. 3 students and 2 graduates from universities with a technical background.

Tested BPMN Processes

The research was based on participants running eye tracking tests relating to typical real-life situations by focusing on documenting the processes involved in real-life testing of the below areas.

Ordering Flight Tickets

The order process in the Air ordering ticket consists of the following steps:

Ordering Burger

The order process in the Burger Restaurant Process consists of the following steps:

Ordering New Electrical Devices (tv, pc, etc.) in E-commerce

The process of ordering new electrical devices from Amazon consists of the following steps:

3.1 Eye Tracking Testing Focus

The passage of participants through the process models is depicted using heat maps. The point at which the participant stops (slows down) is colored red. This creates a map of the areas where the user's attention is engaged. These are probably hard mental operations.

The above procedural BPMNs were also submitted to the parties. We asked questions about whether each sub-step was simple, whether they were able to dilute it, or whether there was any difficulty in understanding. The aim was to discover which symbols or workflows were difficult to understand.

In general, the participants had no significant problems during testing. The models were relatively simple and the participants had a good understanding of the purpose of the testing. They all completed the tasks depending on the intellectual ability of each participant.

Table 1. Cognitive walkthrough - frequency of a usability success, errors or unclear operations in Air ticket ordering

Step	Number of successful	Errors	Unclear operation
Start	-		
Book flight	5		
Type a ticket variant (one way or return)	5		
Destination date and airline class (Economy or Business class)	3	2	
Search for flights	5		
Select cheapest ticket	5		
Confirm selection	5		
Customer information	4		1
Detail confirmation	5		
Proceed to payment	5		
Select Payment options	4	1	
Reserve and pay later	3		2
Reservation completed	1	1	3
Pay and Check-out	5		
End	—		

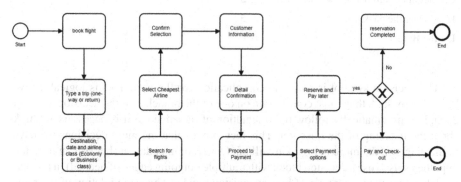

Fig. 9. Ordering flight ticket BPMN, showing all the processes involved

It can be said that the workflows with Diamond symbols showed a lot of hot colors. This is indicative of the fact that the participants were thinking about how to decide how to proceed and retrospectively saw the differences between their options. Thus, it can be said that processes involving decision-making require more focus on recognizing, processing information, and making the subsequent decision (which is probably not a big surprise).

Table 2. Cognitive walkthrough - frequency of a usability success, errors or unclear operations Burger restaurant

Step	Number of successful	Errors	Unclear operation
Hungary for good BG	-		
Choose a BG	5		
Enter an ODR	5		
Request PM	5		
Choose PT	5		
Pay with Card	5		
Pay with Cash	5		
Store Money in the Cash Drawer	4	1	
Activate Payment Terminal (POS)	4		1
Pass the Bill to Cust	5		
Bill with an order number (Message)	4	1	
Grill a Burger	5		
Turn the Burger Over	5		
Place Meat to Bun and Complete by Recipe	5		
Pack the Burger to Paper	5		
Notify the order Complete	5		
Ask for burger	5		
Check Order Number on Customer Bill	5		
Hand Over the package	5		
Eat the Burger	-		

The decision symbol is a visible complication for the user. This is logical, as we have already said, they must concentrate on one of the branches of the decision. It is not enough to pragmatically follow the orientation of the edge but it is necessary to think about the meaning of the question. This fact implies that the more decisions we have in the diagram, the more complex it will be. Our recommendation (but still an untested hypothesis) is to use a decision block with multiple outgoing edges (if needed) in process models rather than a cascade of binary decision blocks. This is a violation of the rules for creating block diagrams, defined in the early days of structured programming.

In some cases, the cascade of decisions makes sense. This is the case when decision making cannot be unified. For example: "do you want to pay by card or cash" and "vegetarian or standard". Here it is not possible to create a factually transparent condition that connects the two choices. However, in the case of payments, e.g. "You wish to pay by A) card, B) cash, C) mobile payment, D) resist payment", it is possible. The decision will be considerably simpler than a sequence of binary decisions, see: "Pay by card Yes, half if Not pay by cash, if Not... Etc." If the process designer is taught to follow

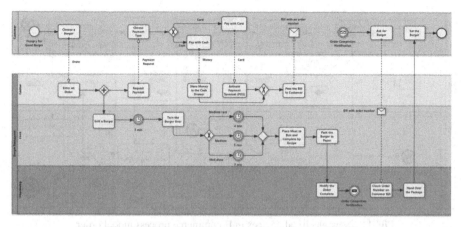

Fig. 10. Ordering Burger from the restaurant, BPMN

Table 3. Cognitive walkthrough - frequency of a usability success, errors or unclear operations Amazon order

Step	Number of successful	Errors	Unclear operation
Customer	-		
Show cart items	5		
Validate cart	4		1
Fill customer information	3		2
Fill shipping address	2	3	
Check deliverability	5		
Fill billing information	5		
Select shipping mode	4		1
Check shipping mode for address	5		
Validate order	3	1	1
Payment	2	2	1
Register order	3		2
Notify Clerk	1	1	3
End the message	-		

the standards of structured programming and "properly designed programs", then his models will be noticeable and easy to use. Recall the following rules: "jumping out of the loop (iteration) is not allowed" and "it is never possible to enter the loop(iteration) body".

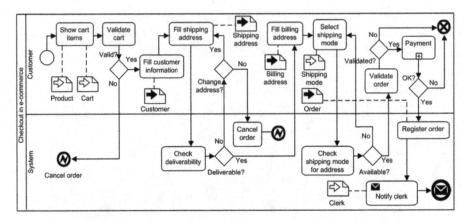

Fig. 11. New electrical devices in E-commerce process model order

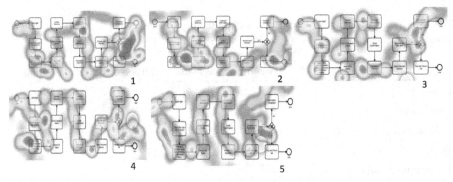

Fig. 12. Ticket order – hard mental operation

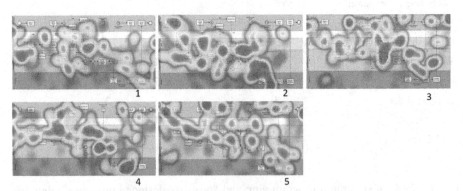

Fig. 13. Burger order - hard mental operation

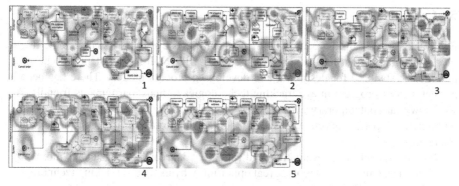

Fig. 14. Ordering new electronic devices - hard mental operation

The technology used has been demonstrated and we are confident that it can be used to assess the quality of the process models in terms of their illustrativeness. The process designer should think about the number of decisions, nesting and general skipping between swimmlines, as this makes the process model less clear and it is really a question of whether it makes any real sense, reps. Whether the same thing could not be designed more simply.

4 Discussion

In general, there is always the question of how telling the number of participants in our usability study is in terms of quantitative measures. Jacob Nielsen [10] shows in his work that effectively 5 participants find 75 percent of usability errors. From this perspective, our method is valid. However, from another angle, it is debatable whether the usability test approach is appropriate for BPMN in particular. We argue [7–9] that it is. The qualitative study conducted here confirms the results we present [7, 9]. However, we now turn to the question of whether decision elements introduce yet other influential characteristics for human perception. Arguably, we can say that a model with fewer decision blocks will be more readable. But the question arises, what about a model where there is simply a lot of decision making? How can we make it clearer? A typical programmer switch operation won't help. So, is nesting the way to go? But that has its pitfalls see [8]. The hypothesis, which is not verified but may come to mind, is whether the solution is not a decision block with more edges than 2. Yes, we have not removed the diamond symbol, but neither have we displayed it more than once according to the standard (the decision is supposed to be binary, i.e. only two edges, TRUE x FALSE). So this area still needs to be studied.

We can also notice measurement inaccuracies, probably caused by poor calibration of the webcam. This is shown by the recordings that had hot colors in the blank areas. However, we can say that this inaccuracy can be mitigated in future studies by a better eye-tracking system.

5   Conclusion

Eye tracking can help us record what catches a user's eye on a visual display. It can give invaluable insight into the process model by BPMN. It has a potential to become an industry standard for designing and developing process models. There has been a perfect start of progress in eye tracking technologies to make participants friendly. As we know that contemporary eye trackers can collect data unobtrusively and remotely without asking participants to wear special tools because tools can affect the participant's interaction.

Moreover, Collecting, evaluating, and validating data can be an easier and more intuitive interface. Currently there is a great opportunity by using eye tracking technologies on mobile devices through the front camera.

Eye tracking can play a significant role in designing successful and effective process models by BPMN and it has the potential to become an industry standard in best practices. On the other hand, BPMN notation is most likely targeted to the participant who is interested in applied computer science. Beside this, it offers process flow tracking, which is advantageous for step-by-step process-by-process without the need to understand it [7–9].

References

1. BPMN Introduction and History. Trisotech (23 Jan. 2022), trisotech.com. https://www.trisot ech.com/bpmn-introduction-and-history/ (Accessed 15 December 2021)
2. Kocbek, M., Jošt, G., Heričko, M., Polančič, G.: Business process model and notation: The current state of affairs. Comput. Sci. Inform. Syst. **12**(2) (2015)
3. Hassen, M.B., Keskes, M., Turki, M., Gargouri, F.: BPMN 4KM: design and implementation of a BPMN extension for modelling the knowledge perspective of sensitive business processes. Proc. Comput. Sci. **121**, 1119–1134 (2017)
4. International Organisation for Standardisation (ISO). Information technology-Object Management Group Business Process Model and Notationn (2013)
5. Martínez-Salvador, B., Marcos, M., Riano, D.: An algorithm for guideline transformation: from BPMN to SDA. Proc. Comput. Sci. **63**, 244–251 (2015)
6. Lucidchart. What is Business Process Modelling Notation?)2016). https://www.lucidchart. com/pages/bpmn/#section_1 (Accessed 24 February 2022)
7. Pavlicek, J., Rod, M., Pavlickova, P.: Usability evaluation of business process modeling standards – BPMN and BORM case study. In: Polyvyanyy, A., Rinderle-Ma, S. (eds.) CAiSE 2021. LNBIP, vol. 423, pp. 93–104. Springer, Cham (2021). https://doi.org/10.1007/978-3-030-79022-6_9
8. Pavlicek, J., Hronza, R., Pavlickova, P., Jelinkova, K.: The business process model quality metrics. In: Pergl, R., Lock, R., Babkin, E., Molhanec, M. (eds.) Enterprise and Organizational Modeling and Simulation, pp. 134–148. Springer International Publishing, Cham (2017). https://doi.org/10.1007/978-3-319-68185-6_10
9. Pavlicek, J., Pavlickova, P.: Methods for evaluating the quality of process modelling tools. In: Pergl, R., Babkin, E., Lock, R., Malyzhenkov, P., Merunka, V. (eds.) EOMAS 2018. LNBIP, vol. 332, pp. 171–177. Springer, Cham (2018). https://doi.org/10.1007/978-3-030-00787-4_12
10. Nielsen, J.: Usability Engineering (Interactive Technologies). Morgan Kaufmann Publisher (1993), ISBN-10: 0125184069

ANP Model as a Support to Decide the Project Management Style

Matej Brnka$^{(\boxtimes)}$, Petra Pavlickova , Jan Rydval , and Josef Pavlicek

Faculty of Economics and Management, Department of Systems Engineering, Czech University of Life Sciences Prague, Kamýcká 129, 165 21, Prague, Czech Republic
{brnka,pavlickovap,rydval,pavlicek}@pef.czu.cz

Abstract. Agile methods in project management are trending as a reaction to the growing and changing business environment. Choosing a proper approach to managing a project is difficult. Many criteria need to be considered. Nowadays, two main approaches to project management are used -agile and waterfall. In the waterfall approach, project phases are in sequence. It means that the customer gets results at the end of the project. Agile methods are based on iterations and increments. The customer is involved in the whole project and provides feedback on the incremental product.

This paper discusses creating an Analytic Network Process (ANP) model, which can provide multi-criteria decision-making. In this paper, clusters and relations are established. Clusters composition comes out on the international project management standard PRINCE2® Agile, Agile Manifesto and SCRUM Guide. Clusters include project management triangle (or hexagon), team characteristics (location, working style and communication) and team members' characteristics (T–Shape, Pi–Shape, I–Shape, X–Shape).

Keywords: Agile methodologies · Analytic network process · Clusters project management · Project · Relations

1 Introduction

Software engineering is a knowledge-intensive process that involves gathering requirements, design, development, testing, maintenance, management, and project coordination [1]. Computers and other smart devices commonly used today are unusable without software. Software development requires a concentrated effort generated by a team of people that needs to be managed [2]. In traditional methodologies (e.g., waterfall), project managers plan and predict all details before the project starts. This is almost impossible in the IT field because the customer does not know all the requirements [1, 3]. Also, non-IT companies (e.g., banks) are transforming their structure to agile using, for example, Spotify, SAFe, and other methodologies to benefit from the agile approach. The most significant benefit is an incremental increase repeated in cycles [3]. Because of that, management can make changes during development with minimal costs. Many organizations have already implemented an agile approach to projects, especially in North America and Europe, not only in IT [4].

© The Author(s), under exclusive license to Springer Nature Switzerland AG 2023
E. Babkin et al. (Eds.): MOBA 2023, LNBIP 488, pp. 65–79, 2023.
https://doi.org/10.1007/978-3-031-45010-5_6

A more realistic approach that considers learning, innovation, and change as they occur throughout product development is what gave rise to the agile family of development approaches. Agile development practices place more emphasis on creating usable software than on spending a lot of time establishing detailed specifications in the beginning. Agile development prioritizes cross-functional teams with autonomy over large hierarchies and functional compartmentalization. Additionally, it emphasizes quick iteration while incorporating ongoing client feedback [5].

With Analytic Network Process (ANP), we can prefer objectives and participate in various objectives and decision-making across several sectors. Cheng used ANP for construction projects [6]. In project management, strategic planning, and marketing research used Rydval [7]; Havazik [8]. A decision network is used to represent the decision problem. ANP includes interdependencies and relationships between network elements from different levels of the hierarchy and between elements of the same levels of the hierarchy [9]. Thus, in this respect, it is a generalization of the analytic hierarchy process (for more information on AHP, see Saaty [10]). By considering many different factors and their interrelationships, ANP improves the quality of decision-making.

This paper discusses constructing an ANP model to recommend whether to choose a more or less classical project management approach (waterfall) or to what extent to involve agility or its elements in project management. The decision is made based on the proposed clusters, decision elements and their relations. The results of this paper is to design and discuss the ANP model.

2   Materials and Methods

2.1   Agile Methods

IT professionals started working on new approaches to develop software. As a result of their work, there were a set of new development methodologies. They met in 2001 at a conference in Utah, and they created the Agile Manifesto. Agile authors created their methodologies on four principles: individuals and interactions over processes and tools, working software over documentation, customer collaboration over contract negotiation, and responding to change according to plan [11].

Agile methodologies focus on dynamics and interaction within the development teams, including a customer representative rather than extensive planning and documentation [12]. Because the representative from the customer is required for constant communication, agile methods are more suitable for smaller-scale projects.

Unlike traditional methods, agile methodologies are used in the environment, where specifications and customer requirements constantly evolve. The agile development process occurs in cycles that include analysis, design, testing, and deployment to production phases [12]. The most popular agile development methodologies include Scrum, Extreme Programming, Feature-Driven Development and Crystal Methods.

2.2   Differences Between the Agile Methods and Traditional Methods

The agile approach is based on the principle that we have a resource (financial, human) and time to complete the project. Requirements are changing during the time based on frequent communication with the customer, which is a part of the development team. On the other hand, the traditional approach lies in fixed requirements because they are gathered at the beginning of the project. Costs and time are estimated and may be changed over time [13].

Agile methods were originally designed for smaller-scale projects, where synchronization of activities is not as necessary as it is in larger projects. The most significant benefit of agile methods is when a customer has no idea about the outcome because he can make changes after sprints (approx. 14 days). Traditional approaches are suitable for larger-scale projects because all requirements are specified initially, and communication with a customer is not so important [12, 14, 15].

Traditional approaches rely on documentation, which is the primary source of communication. It includes all requirements, specifications, design, development, and testing plans. Customer participation is primarily required in the first phase of requirements specification, during milestones, and in the final and over of the finished work [4]. In agile approaches, communication with the customer is continuous because he is a member of the team. In the beginning, critical requirements are specified, and others are defined as the customer comes up with them during the development and use of the software [1, 4, 12].

Agile methods are built on trust between team members and the customer. Success and responsibility lie on each team member. There are used methods, for example, pair programming, in which an older developer teaches a younger one, standup meetings, where everyone can share problems, and the other team members help to solve them. Agile methods have decentralized decisions that take place within the team, where more experienced programmers guide and coach less experienced ones. Traditional methods are the exact opposite: formal status reports, centralized decisions, and direct managerial oversight [1, 4, 13].

2.3 Agile Frameworks

Agile frameworks such as Scrum or Extreme Programming are primally defined for small teams and minor projects. These frameworks are thriving on the team level. However, companies want to benefit from agile advantages in more significant projects or at higher organizational levels. By this need Scaling Agile Frameworks have been created. Only a few of these frameworks are used in practice for example SAFe, Scrum of Scrums, and LeSS (Large Scaled Scrum) [16].

2.4 Agile Hexagon

PRINCE2® Agile considers 6 aspects needed to be controlled and managed: time, cost, benefits, risk, quality, and scope. Typical variables for waterfall are time and cost and typical variables in agile are quality and scope (Fig. 1).

PRINCE2® Agile [17] gives guidance using tolerance levels for the six aspects in terms of what should be fixed, and which ones should vary - we are using flex.

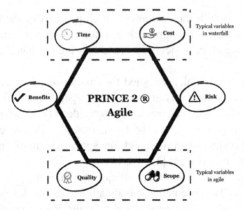

Fig. 1. PRINCE2® Agile – What to fix and what to flex, course materials, own processing.

According to these variables in waterfall is fixed time and cost and flexed scope and quality and for agile is fixed time and cost and flexed scope and quality. This we can see in Fig. 2. Agile Hexagon. It is not that fixed variables can never flexed but they have tolerances set to zero and would be potentially adept to management by exception if these will exceed. Based on this Agile hexagon, the clusters for the ANP method were determined in the results section.

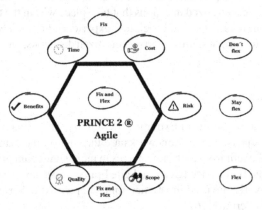

Fig. 2. Agile Hexagon: Tayllorcox, source: PRINCE2® Agile [17]

2.5 Analytic Network Process (ANP)

Deciding whether to lead a project in a classical (waterfall) or agile way is difficult. We need many criteria to consider taking such a decision. Thus, it is a multi-criteria decision-making problem. Multi-criteria decision-making can be challenging because of the many criteria that need to be considered and the different levels of importance (weights) of these criteria. Multi-criteria decision-making is also challenging because of the uncertainty and vagueness, which can affect the quality of the decision outcome. Decision-making is also challenging because of the different stakeholders who may have different priorities, objectives, or interests. The importance of individual stakeholders' subjective preferences and personal attitudes is another essential element of multi-criteria decision-making, which is why sophisticated mathematical processes are often used to support such complex decisions. One of them is the analytic network process (ANP).

ANP is a mathematical method that helps in the decision-making process and allows to structure of complex decision problems into relational networks, including interdependencies and relationships not only between network elements from different levels of the hierarchy but also interdependencies and relationships between elements of the same levels of the hierarchy [9]. Using ANP, it is possible to prioritize different objectives and participate in decision-making in many sectors, such as project management, strategic planning and marketing research. ANP allows for estimating the priorities (weights) of different network elements in the decision-making process, such as criteria, and thus evaluates and compares different variants of decisions. ANP also allows consideration of interdependencies between elements (different decision-making factors) of the same level [18], which can be helpful when deciding on complex issues. Thus, in this respect, it is a generalization of the analytic hierarchy process (for more information on AHP, see Saaty, 2000, [10]). By considering many different factors and their interrelationships, ANP improves the quality of decision-making. ANP can be considered a helpful tool for decision-makers in project management [7] so it can also be used to select the appropriate form of project management. This means that ANP can be used in decision-making, whether to choose a classical (waterfall) or agile way of project management.

The basic elements of the ANP method are following:

- The first step of ANP is based on the creation of a network which describes dependency among decision elements.
- In the second step pairwise comparisons of the elements within the clusters and among the clusters are performed.
- The third step consists of the supermatrix construction.
- In the fourth step the Limit Matrix is computed and global preferences (weights) of decision elements are obtained.

2.6   ANP Example

To illustrate how the ANP method works, consider the following decision problem. A decision-maker in the IT project area is faced with the question of how large a project (development) team is appropriate for him depending on the suitability of different types of team members suitable for different-sized project teams. The decision problem can be divided into two basic aspects: 1) The project team size aspect (Small – **S**, Medium – **M**, and Large – **L** size) and 2) The team member type aspect (I –Shape – **I**, T – Shape – **T**, Pi – Shape – **Pi** person). In a classical AHP view of this decision problem, the individual aspects would either have to be viewed separately and de facto solve two separate decision problems (problem structure shown in Fig. 3 above left), or the personality aspect could be inserted into the problem hierarchy above the team size as an intermediate evaluation step.

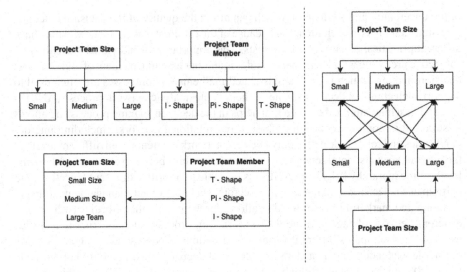

Fig. 3. AHP and ANP structure

However, the reality of this decision problem is different because the individual decision elements are interdependent, which is impossible to represent in a classical hierarchically structured decision problem. Therefore, regarding Team Size and Types of Team Members, it is necessary to use a network structure for the decision problem (shown in Fig. 3 on the right). According to the first step of the ANP, this representation can be simplified by using clusters with their decision elements. In this case, a Team Size cluster with three decision elements and a Team Member type cluster also with three decision elements (shown in Fig. 3 on the bottom left).

When quantifying the ANP model (the second step of the ANP algorithm), the decision maker pairwise compares the importance of the individual decision elements in the first cluster regarding the individual decision elements of the second cluster. Thus, for example, in terms of the I – Shape team member, the decision maker assesses the appropriateness of the team size, i.e. how large a team is suitable for the I – Shape team member to work in. According to Saaty [17], for quantitative pairwise evaluation, the decision maker mainly uses odd preference degrees (1,3,5,7,9, where 1 means equivalence and 9 means absolute preference) but even degrees (2,4,6,8) can also be used. Inverted values are used to express that the decision maker does not prefer something. In our example, where the decision maker for the I – Shape team member is comparing small team size with medium team size, the value 1/5 expresses that he does not strongly prefer medium size over small size. The decision maker prefers medium over small size, expressed by a value of 5 below the main diagonal of the matrix (shown in Fig. 4 on the left). From the preference matrix filled in this way, according to Saaty [17], a supermatrix can be constructed (the third step of the algorithm), and the final preferences of each decision element in the limit matrix can be computed (the fourth step of the ANP algorithm).

	S	M	L	Priority
S	1	1/5	1/9	0.7219
M	5	1	1/5	0.2271
L	9	5	1	0.0510

Decision node	Normal Value
I	0.2153
T	0.4295
Pi	0.3553
S	0.3379
M	0.4336
L	0.2285

Fig. 4. Saaty's pairwise comparison (left), Table of final preferences (right)

In our case, when the decision maker faces the problem of choosing the appropriate size of the project team depending on the suitability of different types of project members for different-sized work teams, the decision maker obtains the following results; values for team sizes are: small 0.3379, medium 0.4336, and large 0.2285 (shown in Fig. 4 on the right). Normalizing these values within each cluster, the decision maker obtains the following results: small 33.79%, medium 43.36%, and large 22.85%, which indicates that the team size should be medium or smaller, and at the same time, with respect to the results from project team member personality type, the decision maker should choose mostly T – Shape personality.

Real decision situations require constructing a far more complex decision model structure and completing far more extensive pairwise comparisons, but the principle of the ANP algorithm is identical.

3 Results

To create a model to support the decision on which type of project management to choose. The model will recommend whether to choose a more or less classical project management approach (waterfall) or to what extent to involve agility or its elements in project management. The model will give a percentage value of the degree of project management using elements of one or the other management method. Therefore, building a decision model in the form of a relational network of individual decision elements was necessary. It is crucial to identify the individual clusters of the network, including their decision elements.

The composition of individual clusters is based on the chapter Materials and Methods. Cluster Project Scope, Project Time and Project Cost are based on the project triangle. The Project Triangle extended into a Project Hexagon, according to PRINCE2® Agile [17], resulting in another cluster of Project Benefits. Furthermore, based on the PRINCE2® Agile and the Agilometer methodology [17], we added the clusters Project Member, Project Team Working Style and Project Team Communication to the model. Based on knowledge of Agile Manifesto [19], we added the cluster Project Delivery Methods and Project Team Size to the model. From our experience in project management, the clusters Project Type and Project Complexity were cut into the model.

The main objective of the ANP model is to find the preference of the project management approach, whether to use agile methodologies or the traditional approach. Based on the input data - preferences of individual decision criteria, which may show inter-relationships between elements within the same or different hierarchical levels of the decision network, the model will recommend an approach to project management from the perspective of individual clusters. The decision maker will determine preferences within each cluster, and the model output will recommend how to manage the project.

3.1 Clusters Description

Cluster Project Time - Project time can be either fixed or flexed (variable or flexible), and project teams work accordingly. Fixed time means that teams work in predefined time intervals (e.g. 14 days, i.e. one sprint), and then we can calculate how much work can be done in a given time using methods (e.g. Burndown Chart). Flexible time is the opposite; each project phase can take a different amount of time (e.g. analysis, development).

Cluster Project Scope - Project Scope defines what is to be produced within the project. We included the cluster because the results of a waterfall project cannot be changed during the project (or only with great difficulty). The project scope can be fixed or flexible (flexible). A fixed scope means that we already know what is to be done when we start the project, and it cannot be changed during the project. On the other hand, we can change the project deliverables arbitrarily over time and customer feedback with a flexible scope, which is what agile methodologies take advantage of.

Cluster Project Cost - The cluster cost of a project is another significant cluster and influences whether a project is successful or unsuccessful. Costs can be either fixed or flexed. Fixed costs mean that they cannot change during the project (or during some stage of the project). If costs can change during the project, they are flexed. Agile methodologies have fixed costs, so frequent changes in project scope do not increase costs. In contrast, the waterfall approach uses flexed costs and changes as needed during the project.

Cluster Project Properties - This cluster includes other project properties according to the project hexagon; see chapter Agile Hexagon 2.4 Agile Hexagon. These properties can also influence how the project is to be managed. For example, the decision maker may prefer (or his preferences may be balanced) quality over risk, and similar logic can be applied to all combinations within the cluster. Benefits imply a measurable improvement in project outcomes as a benefit to one or more stakeholders. Quality describes what the final product must be. It leads to a reduction in costs in the subsequent life cycles of the final product. Risks are unexpected events that positively or negatively affect the project's progress [17].

Cluster Project Complexity - This cluster defines the coherence of the project concerning existing results. This can influence the decision on which approach to take to manage the project. The more complex the project is in relation to a Project Type, the more planning and implementation of the final outputs. Thus, a waterfall approach to project management would be more appropriate. Conversely, for less complex projects, it is more appropriate to use agile methods [20].

Cluster Project Type - In this cluster, we consider what type of project is being delivered. According to Agile Manifesto [19], agile methodologies are designed primarily for software development. However, they can also be used in other industries where frequent feedback from the customer or regular incremental evaluation is necessary to keep the project moving in the right direction. In our model, we consider projects from different industries, namely IT, design, industrial, marketing, and research projects. Agile methodologies are more appropriate for IT or marketing projects, whereas a waterfall approach is more likely to be used in construction projects.

Cluster Project Team Member - This cluster considers what type of workers are available. According to PRINCE2® Agile [17], it is advisable to have individual members within agile teams with a focus on multiple areas of expertise (e.g. for IT projects development, analytics) so that team members can represent each other and communicate clearly. For waterfall projects, given their phases, we can always allocate staff with specialization in a particular area according to the project schedule. I-Shaped people have a single and deep specialty of expertise area. They have limited knowledge of different disciplines and prefer to work on a single job. T-Shaped people have specialized skills and general knowledge in other disciplines. Pi-Shaped people have expertise in two or more knowledge areas and general knowledge. X-Shaped people have unique human capabilities and can learn and adapt to a new environment.

Cluster Project Team Location - Cluster Project Team Location defines whether team members and the customer are geographically in one or more locations. In agile methodologies, customer involvement and communication are critical, both with the customer and between team members. This cluster has only two elements - Virtual Team or Onsite Team. The significance of the Onsite Team is that the team can meet in person at one place when needed.

Cluster Delivery Method - This cluster describes how the final product of the project is delivered. For agile methodologies, the final product's continuous delivery (increment) is typical. Subsequently, the customer gives feedback, and then the final product is modified according to it. Continuous delivery is not possible for some types of projects, leading to a waterfall approach to project management.

Cluster Project Team Size - The cluster also includes team size in the model. Agile methodologies are characterized by less cross-functional and self-management, with no sub-teams or hierarchies. A scrum team should have at most ten members to be maximally effective [21]. For our model, we have defined the following elements to determine preferences: Large, Medium, and Small Team Sizes. As a small team is considered team with less than 10 members, medium team 10–39 members and large team 40 + members [4, 20].

Cluster Project Communication - Since communication within the team is central to agile methods, it is therefore included in the model in this cluster. The different elements of this cluster are Cooperation Communication Style and Directive Communication Style. Directive Communication Style is based on the manager's commands of what or how to do within the final product. Agile methodologies enforce Cooperation Communication Style, where the team agrees on the outcome and the solution process.

Cluster Project Team Working Style - The last cluster is the way the team works. The team can collaborate on the final product and help each other solve the problem. Collaboration is rather typical for agile methodologies, where it is the mainstay. On the other hand, individual members may work in an individualistic manner, which can lead to inconsistent results from individual members (Fig. 5).

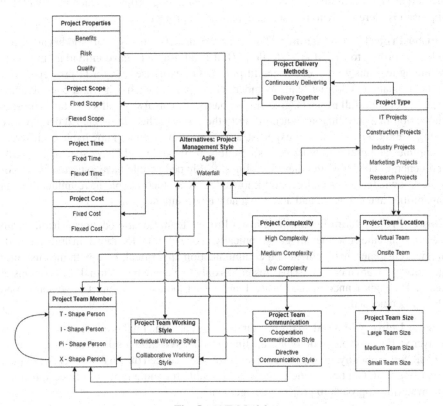

Fig. 5. ANP Model

3.2 Relations Description

The relationships between clusters determine the values of the evaluator pairwise comparisons. Thus, the evaluator determines whether to use an agile or waterfall approach to project management, for example, in the Project Time cluster. Clusters can have the following relations: input, output, and self-loop.

Cluster Project Time - This cluster has only one relation directly linked to the decision alternatives. We ask from the from point of view of each element of the cluster. This logic is applied to all constraints. The relation describes whether it is better to run the project agile or waterfall from a fixed time perspective. Similarly, in terms of flexible time, is it better to run the project agile or waterfall? However, this constraint can also be approached from the reverse point of view of each element of the Project Management Style cluster. So, from an agile project management point of view, is it better to use flex or fixed time? From a waterfall project management perspective, is fixed or flex time better? Fixed time is more suitable for agile methodologies, whereas flex time tends to be more towards the traditional way of project management.

Cluster Project Scope - This cluster has only one direct relation to the decision alternatives. The relation describes whether it is better to run the project waterfall or agile in terms of fixed scope. Similarly, whether it is better from a flexed scope perspective to lead a projected waterfall or agile. Since the relation is two-sided, we examine whether it is better to have a fixed or flexed scope from an agile project management point of view. Similarly, then whether it is better to have a fixed scope or a flexible scope in terms of waterfall project management. The fixed scope is necessary for waterfall-managed projects, and agile methodologies use flexible scope.

Cluster Project Cost - Let us ask in terms of Project Costs (fixed or flexed). We are interested in the appropriate approach to project management (agile or waterfall). For example, whether for fixed costs, it is appropriate to have the project managed agile or waterfall.

Cluster Project Properties - If we ask from the point of view of Project Properties (benefits, risk, quality), we are interested in the appropriate way of project management (agile or waterfall). For example, whether a quality preference is appropriate for an agile or waterfall approach to project management. The same then applies to reverse the same logic as above. For example, whether we prefer any of the mentioned project management characteristics for the agile approach.

Cluster Project Complexity - If we ask about Project Complexity (high, medium, low), we are interested in the appropriate team size (Large, Medium, Small Team Size) for different types of complexity. Similar logic applies in terms of Project Team Communication, Project Team Member and Project Team Location. Regarding Project Complexity, we are interested in the appropriate Project Management Style (waterfall or agile). At the same time, regarding Project Management Style (agile or waterfall), we ask how complex a project should be managed with which methodology.

Cluster Project Type - In terms of Project Type (IT, Construction, Industry, Marketing, Research Projects), we are interested in the appropriate way of project delivery (Continuously or Together) and Project Team Location (Virtual or Onsite Team). We are also interested in the appropriate project management method (Agile or Waterfall) for different types of projects. This principle also applies in reverse, using similar logic as mentioned above.

Cluster Project Team Member - This cluster has only input relations and self-loop relation. We ask, for example, in terms of team size (Large, Medium, Small) what the team members should be (T-Shape, I-Shape, Pi-Shape, X-Shape). The same logic applies to Project Team Communication, Project Team Location and Project Complexity. Self-loop linkage goes back to personality type. It models a situation where another team member must replace the absence of one specific team member. In this case, the question is which of the other team members (in terms of personality type) can best replace the missing member.

Cluster Project Team Location - If we ask from the point of view of Project Team Location (Virtual or Onsite), we are interested in what kind of project team members (T-Shape, I-Shape, Pi-Shape, X-Shape) we should have for different kinds of Project Team Locations. Similar logic can be used for Project Management Style, i.e. if we have such teams available, for example, what approach to project management should we use? This logic also applies in reverse, so if we have an Agile project, for example, we should have an Onsite Team.

Cluster Delivery Method - Regarding Project Delivery Methods (Continuously or Together at once), we are interested in which method we should use to manage the project. At the same time, we are also interested if we have, for example, Agile Project Management, then what method should we use to deliver the project.

Cluster Project Team Size - If we ask about Project Team Size (Large, Medium, Small), we are interested in the appropriate project management method (Agile or Waterfall) for different team sizes. For example, if we have a Small Team Size, is it better to manage the project Agile or Waterfall? This logic applies in reverse by the same principle as stated above. Regarding team size, we are also interested in what the team members should be (T-Shape, I-Shape, Pi-Shape, X-Shape) for different team sizes.

Cluster Project Communication - Regarding Project Communication (Cooperation or Directive Communication Style), we are interested in the appropriate way to manage the project (Agile or Waterfall) based on different communication methods. This logic applies in reverse; when we ask from the point of view of Project Management Style (agile or waterfall), we are interested in how the team should communicate. We also ask from the Project Team Communication point of view what the members of the project team should be like (T-Shape, I-Shape, Pi-Shape, X-Shape) based on the different ways of communication.

Cluster Project Team Working Style - Let us ask from the point of view of the Project Team Working Style (Individual or Collaborative). We are interested in the appropriate project management method (Agile or Waterfall) for different Project Team Working Styles. This logic also applies in reverse. If we ask about Project Management Style, we are interested in how the team should work together. We are also asking whether, from the Project Team Working Style perspective, we are interested in the appropriate project team members for different ways of working together.

The above-discussed clusters, including their essential decision elements and defined relationships, shape our proposed decision model to support the decision of what type of project management to choose. The individual decision elements can thus be viewed as de facto decision criteria in a multi-criteria decision problem.

The advantage of the presented decision model is the possibility to modify the content of the individual clusters to a given decision situation or decision-maker. In this respect, the ANP method is flexible and suitable for project management, where different stakeholder groups may have different interests.

4 Discussion

Choosing the appropriate project management style can be complex, and there are many criteria to consider selecting the appropriate Project Management Style. We use the ANP method to decision support which Project Management Style should be chosen. The crucial part of ANP is to structure the complex decision problem into a relational network containing clusters and decision nodes. The construction of the clusters in the model is based on the Materials and Methods chapter. We used the PRINCE2® Agile methodology principles [17], Scrum Guide [21] and Agile Manifesto [19]. We built the ANP model. According to Ziemba [22], ANP model seems more appropriate than the AHP model in such situation. In some projects, it may be appropriate to use both approaches to project management, which is not considered in our model. For example, one phase of the project is managed in an agile way, while another is managed in a waterfall approach. For example, the development phase will be managed in an agile way, whereas in the case of the subsequent phase of obtaining certification, a waterfall approach is more appropriate. This approach has been presented in Project, Agile and Leadership Conference in Prague at 2021 [23].

In the following research phase, we will conduct a pilot study using the model proposed above to determine the preferences of its elements. This pilot study will be a small-scale study before the primary research in defining the various criteria for selecting the project management approach since it is very challenging to maintain consistency in the choice of pairwise comparisons of the decision maker. His decisions are often inconsistent if the decision maker is asked to make pairwise comparisons in third and higher-order matrices. Since the decision maker is not expected to re-evaluate pairwise comparisons constantly, this inconsistency must be resolved in other ways. A new way of ensuring consistency was introduced by Hlavatý and Brožová [24], whose approach is based on a nonlinear optimization model. They found a way to adjust the values of the matrix in such a way that the original information contained in the pairwise comparison is preserved while achieving acceptable inconsistency.

5 Conclusion

This paper aimed to build an ANP model to support whether to manage the project agile or waterfall. We built the model with the following clusters: Project Time, Project Scope, Project Cost, Project Befenits, Project Complexity, Project Type, Project Team Member, Project Team Location, Delivery Method, Project Team Size, Project Communication Style, and Project Team Working Style. We also discussed the importance of each cluster and the relationships between them. Using multi-criteria decision-making methods, we could recommend which project management (agile or waterfall) method to choose. The ANP model seems suitable for this decision-making method, and the clusters are appropriately chosen. In the following research, we will conduct a pilot study where the ANP model will be mathematically calculated and provide recommendations for selecting an appropriate project management method. Subsequently, the main study will be conducted, where we will collect data and address the consistency of pairwise comparisons.

Acknowledgements. The results and knowledge included herein have been obtained owing to support from the following institutional grant. Internal grant agency of the Faculty of Economics and Management, Czech University of Life Sciences Prague, grant no. 2022A0009.

References

1. Chau, T., Maurer, F., Melnik, G.: Knowledge sharing: agile methods vs. Tayloristic methods. In: Proceedings of the Workshop on Enabling Technologies: Infrastructure for Collaborative Enterprises, WETICE, pp. 302–307. IEEE Computer Society (2003). https://doi.org/10.1109/ENABL.2003.1231427
2. Singh Ghuman, S.: International Journal of Computer Science and Mobile Computing SDLC Models-A Survey (2013). www.ijcsmc.com
3. Ciric, D., Lalic, B., Gracanin, D., Tasic, N., Delic, M., Medic, N.: Agile vs. traditional approach in project management: strategies, challenges and reasons to introduce agile. In: Procedia Manufacturing, pp. 1407–1414. Elsevier B.V. (2019). https://doi.org/10.1016/j.promfg.2020.01.314
4. Radhakrishnan, A., Zaveri, J., David, D., Davis, J.S.: The impact of project team characteristics and client collaboration on project agility and project success: an empirical study. Eur. Manag. J. (2021). https://doi.org/10.1016/j.emj.2021.09.011
5. Sutherland, J.: The Scrum Papers (2022). http://jeffsutherland.com/scrumpapers.pdf
6. Cheng, E.W.L., Li, H.: Analytic Network Process Applied to Project Selection. https://doi.org/10.1061/ASCE0733-93642005131:4459
7. Rydval, J., Bartoska, J., Jedlanova, T.: Sensitivity analysis of priorities of project team roles using the ANP model. In: Houda, M., Remes, R. (eds.) Proceedings of the 37th International Conference Mathematical Methods in Economic 2019, pp. 320–325. UNIV South Bohemia Ceske Budejovice, FAC Economics, Ceske Budejovice (2019)
8. Havazik, O., Pavlickova, P., Rydval, J.: Model design for team roles in agile IT projects. In: Vojackova, H. (ed.) Proceedings of the 40th International Conference Mathematical Methods in Economics 2022, pp. 91–97. Coll Polytechnics Jihlava, Tolsteho (2022)
9. Saaty, T.L.: Decision Making with Dependence and Feedback: The Analytic Network Process. RWS (1996)
10. Saaty, T.L.: Fundamentals of the Analytic Hierarchy Process. RWS Publications, Pittsburgh (2000)
11. Hneif, M., Ow, S.H.: Review of Agile Methodologies in Software Development Review of Agile Methodologies in Software Development (2009). https://www.researchgate.net/publication/41392207
12. Balijepally, V., Mahapatra, R., Nerur, S.P.: Assessing personality profiles of software developers in agile development teams. Commun. Assoc. Inf. Syst. **18** (2006). https://doi.org/10.17705/1cais.01804
13. Stober, T., Hansmann, U.: Traditional software development. In: Agile Software Development, pp. 15–33. Springer, Heidelberg (2010). https://doi.org/10.1007/978-3-540-70832-2_2
14. Van Casteren, W.: The waterfall model and the agile methodologies : a comparison by project characteristics. In: Academic Competences in the Bachelor 2 Assignment: Write a Scientific Article on 2 Software Development Models (2017). http://www.thefreedictionary.com/agile
15. Venkatesh, D., Rakhra, M.: Agile adoption issues in large scale organizations: a review. Mater. Today Proc. (2020). https://doi.org/10.1016/j.matpr.2020.11.308
16. Diebold, P., Schmitt, A., Theobald, S.: Scaling Agile – How to Select the Most Appropriate Framework (2018)

17. AXELOS Limited (ed.) PRINCE2 Agile, 1st edn. TSO, The Stationery Office, Norwich (2015)
18. Saaty, T.L.: Decision Making with Dependence and Feedback: The Analytic Network Process. RWS Publications, Pittsburgh (2001)
19. Beck, K., et al.: Manifesto for Agile Software Development (2021)
20. Müller, R., Turner, J.R.: Matching the project manager's leadership style to project type. Int. J. Project Manag. **25**(1), 21–32 (2007). https://doi.org/10.1016/j.ijproman.2006.04.003
21. Schwaber, K., Sutherland, J.: The Scrum Guide The Definitive Guide to Scrum: The Rules of the Game (2020)
22. Ziemba, P.: Inter-criteria dependencies-based decision support in the sustainable wind energy management. Energies (Basel) **12**(4), 749 (2019). https://doi.org/10.3390/en12040749
23. 13th Annual Hybrid Project. Agile & Leadership conference in Prague, Prague, 16 September 2021. https://www.pmkonference.cz/en/2021/. Accessed 09 Apr 2023
24. Hlavaty, R., Brozova, H.: Optimisation approach to dealing with Saaty's inconsistency. In: Vojackova, H. (ed.) Proceedings of the 40th International Conference Mathematical Methods in Economics 2022, pp. 104–109. Coll Polytechnics Jihlava, Tolsteho (2022)

Character Segmentation in the Development of Palmyrene Aramaic OCR

Adéla Hamplová[✉] [ID], David Franc[✉] [ID], and Josef Pavlicek[ID]

Czech University of Life Sciences in Prague, Kamýcká 129, 165 00 Praha-Suchdol, Prague, Czech Republic
{hamplova,francd,pavlicek}@pef.czu.cz

Abstract. In this study, we present the research plan and the segmentation solution in progress for our Palmyrene OCR web and mobile application from sandstone tablet photographs, which will be publicly available on the ml-research.pef.czu.cz web portal in the next steps of the research. In this paper, we compare mathematical segmentation methods with artificial intelligence methods, highlighting the advantages and disadvantages of each solution, and propose a fully automated OCR procedure from photographs using convolutional neural networks exclusively and present a development model of our solution. We also present a partially completed segmentation dataset of the Palmyrene letters to demonstrate the functionality of the proposed procedure. We hope to complete the Palmyrene OCR soon, thus making the writings of ancient Palmyra accessible to the scientific community and the public, signifying progress in the area of Digital Humanities. Since the algorithm is not completely ready yet, we also present its development model here.

Keywords: Artificial Intelligence · Segmentation · Historical Alphabet · Software Development Modelling

1 Introduction

The use of Optical Character Recognition (OCR) has become increasingly important in modern times, enabling the automated processing of scanned documents, handwritten notes, and other images of text. However, to achieve accurate OCR results, it is crucial to first segment the text from the surrounding noise and other elements within the image. In the context of analyzing historical texts, which are not written on paper that can be scanned, developing a reliable OCR algorithm is a challenging task.

In recent years, several historical OCR datasets have been developed (see section: Theoretical overview – Historical OCR in digital humanities), which contain text images and corresponding ground truth segmentations for training and evaluating OCR models.

In this scientific article, we introduce a new segmentation Palmyrene OCR dataset that we have developed and present an analysis of its characteristics and potential applications. Our dataset consists of diverse polygon-labelled images of Palmyrene inscriptions, funerary stelae, and other sandstone tablets with Palmyrene Aramaic texts, provided by

© The Author(s), under exclusive license to Springer Nature Switzerland AG 2023
E. Babkin et al. (Eds.): MOBA 2023, LNBIP 488, pp. 80–95, 2023.
https://doi.org/10.1007/978-3-031-45010-5_7

several museums (see section: Methodology - Data). The photographs include varying handwritings of different colors, sizes, and backgrounds. We believe that this dataset will be a valuable resource for researchers and practitioners working on OCR and related applications, enabling them to develop and test robust and accurate OCR models.

As the OCR algorithm is not finished at the time, a model of the development process is presented here as well, allowing easy to understand and easy to follow steps to complete it in the near future.

2 Theoretical Overview

2.1 SW Development Modelling

Process Management is, to quote [1], nowadays "considered as a new way of managing an organization". According to [2] it is a managerial-economic discipline. The technology of process-oriented management is used here. We can say that process management is actually a set of tools, technologies and methods that are used to design, analyze, validate, approve and manage processes.

The management of an organization, or just in our case the management of a team, is then based on the principles of process mapping. Each process consists of sub-steps or tasks. These have to be executed chronologically or some have to be executed in parallel.

2.2 OCR

Developed first in the mid-20th century, OCR systems are now considered to be one of the most intricate applications of computer vision and image recognition [3]. Essentially, OCR involves identifying patterns that represent alphanumeric or other characters from a digital photograph or PDF scan [4].

The whole process of Optical Character Recognition (OCR) [5] involves the digitization of physical documents such as papers or historical artifacts with inscriptions, through scanning or photographing. The digitized image then undergoes local segmentation to differentiate text from other graphical elements, followed by optional pre-processing to reduce noise and normalize the image. The next step, segmentation or binarization, separates the image into non-text and text parts, and further segments the text into individual characters or parts of characters. The characters are then represented through global, statistical, or geometric representations. Feature extraction is commonly achieved through template matching, based on the distribution of points extracted from the image. OCR systems are trained and recognized through the creation of templates of individual features, using statistical techniques, cluster analysis, or artificial neural networks. Post-processing involves the composition of detected features into words, which are compared with a dictionary and modified for coherence. The final step is the output text in a machine-readable format, which can be further processed through natural language processing systems for tasks such as language translation or text summarization.

2.3 Historical OCR in Digital Humanities

Related Research

The interest in creating historical OCR is constantly rising, as standard historical text analysis needs to be done by experts in the field, who can read and translate the ancient languages. This process is time-consuming and limited to a small number of specialists, therefore automation of this process A cuneiform NLP algorithm was developed by Gordin et al. from hand-written cuneiform transliterations [6], and a cuneiform horizontal stroke detection was developed thereafter [7]. An evaluation tool for Arabic OCR was published in 2017, presenting custom metrics [8], followed by a new Arabic OCR dataset consisting of almost 9000 images in 2018 [9]. A Bangla classification dataset [10] was published in 2020. A team from Bangladesh and Japan developed BengaliNet [11], a classification network for Bengali hand-written characters with an average of 97.5% accuracy. The Persian alphabet recognition dataset [12] was presented in 2020.

Palmyrene OCR Development

Our team has started working on Palmyrene OCR in 2021, at first by creating a classification dataset of hand-written and photographic data. We have implemented the classifier on efficient_lite0 architecture in an Android application presented in CSOC Springer conference [13], followed by presenting a custom optimized classifier for hand-written Palmyrene characters [14]. As photograph classification was not very successful, we used augmentation methods such as keras augmentation and Generative Adversarial Networks and doubled the accuracy [15]. We also created a web application (for which the paper is under review), available at ml-research.pef.czu.cz. There, the photo classification, and hand-written classification is available as well. At the time, the application accepts only one letter at a time as input, so transliterating the whole sandstone tablets take a lot of time. Therefore, we started working at automatic segmentation.

2.4 Contemporary Segmentation Methods

To improve recognition, current OCR research [16] incorporates different systems into a hybrid solution, which lowers the error rate when only one OCR algorithm is utilized. Systems are being created for languages that were previously unavailable, such as Arabic [17], Hindi [18], Japanese [19], and many more, but not Palmyrene Aramaic.

Post-processing techniques are being improved to account for many forms of errors and make automatic corrections [20]. The issues that these systems run into in typical settings are mentioned in a comparison study of existing OCR systems from 2021 [21], but only for Latin OCR herein. One of them is the challenge of identifying letters on a scanned page when they are deformed, blurry, or when whole characters are missing. The necessity to extract numerous distinct features for each character class or to use multiple templates and elastic templates for character classification is caused by font variations, which is another issue. As the letters in the Palmyrene script are carved in sandstone rather than written on paper, it is logical to conclude that both of these concerns will also be relevant in the OCR development of this script. In order to highlight the features of characters from background, it will be important to utilize the proper pre-processing techniques. Additionally, neural networks can be used for feature extraction and classification rather than template matching.

Contemporary OCR system approaches involve complex compositions of mathematical and artificial intelligence methods in each phase of the algorithm. We believe that the development of OCR systems can be simplified given the state of artificial neural networks, and we want to investigate this idea here.

3 Objective

The goal of this step of our research is to automate the reading of Palmyrene inscriptions from a photograph of sandstone tablets or funerary stelae. As Palmyrene Aramaic inscriptions are read right to left, top to bottom, we plan to:

- segment each of the characters from the background using computer vision, namely instance segmentation
- program a script, which will redraw the segmentation predictions to polygons in a blank image
- create a SW development model of our solution

4 Methodology

4.1 Data Acquisition

To get high quality photographs of Palmyrene inscriptions, we have contacted several museums and retrieved available images of sandstone tablets, coins, and funerary reliefs:

- Musée du Louvre [22]
- Archaeological Museum of Palmyra [23] (Fig. 1)
- Virtual Museum of Syria [24]
- British Museum [25]
- Ontario Museum [26].

4.2 Pre-processing

Some of the images had poorly visible inscriptions, therefore, preprocessing in the form of adjusting brightness, contrast and color spectrum of these images was necessary, before uploading to the annotation platform.

4.3 Annotating Segmentation Dataset

The annotation of polygonal labels for instance segmentation was conducted in the online tool Roboflow [27]. Roboflow is a computer vision platform that helps researchers and other users build, train, and also deploy computer vision models, such as classification, object detection, instance or semantic segmentation and more. The platform offers a suite of tools and services designed to simplify the process of creating custom machine

Fig. 1. Example photograph of Palmyrene inscriptions used in the dataset, Archaeological Museum of Palmyra, Inv. 1439/8583; text: ḥb' brt | šmšgrm | br bny bzy l't b'ly | br 'gylw | ḥbl

learning models for image and video analysis. Roboflow allows users to upload their own datasets of images, then pre-process and augment the data after labelling, in order to improve model accuracy. Roboflow also offers APIs and SDKs that enable more granular control over the machine learning process, or the datasets can be exported and used in custom training.

We have created an instance segmentation dataset and used polygonal label tool to create points, that outline each character. There is just one class – character – and each character is later classified by custom classifier in a custom script Draw-Polygon.

4.4 Draw-Polygon Tool Development

We have developed an algorithm for processing and plotting polygons, which are results of YOLOv5 predictions. The polygons are read from a text file, where each polygon is represented as a set of points. The points are parsed, and their x and y coordinates are extracted into separate lists. Each polygon is plotted as a filled shape using matplotlib. The resulting plot is saved as an image and loaded for further processing with PIL. The image is flipped horizontally and resized with antialiasing. A new blank image is created with size 100x100, and the resized image is pasted in the center. The padded image is saved, and the original image is removed.

The input to the tool is in the format 0 (index class of object – in this case there is just one class - character) followed by a list of (x-coordinate y-coordinate). The output images are visible in Fig. 2.

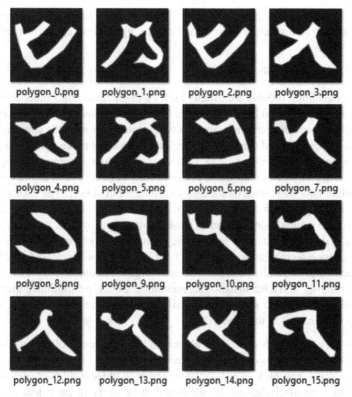

Fig. 2. A sample of output images from Draw-Polygon tool, characters 0: shin, 1: mem, 2: shin, 3: he, 4: samekh, 5: mem, 6: beth, 7: daleth, 8: nun, 9: waw, 10: daleth, 11: beth, 12: gimel, 13: 14: daleth, 15: aleph and 16: waw

4.5   SW Development Modelling

For modeling purposes, the OnLine tool Cardanit BPMN [28] was used. This tool can be used directly in the browser of the computer. It does not need to be installed and a very powerful feature is that it is possible to share the project with another researcher of the team and work on it simultaneously in real time.

BPMN was chosen as the notation for modeling the partial steps of the project. In our case, the chronology is written down as tasks that are carried out in individual years (these are represented by the so-called swimlines). Events that have occurred or will occur (that is, mainly publishing activities) are recorded using textual descriptions. Here we depart from the BPMN notation. We do not use the "event" symbol for them. This is because an "event" is seen as a kind of milestone that performs an action in the process model. In our case, however, it is an external output that does not enter the process model further.

The next model is a block diagram (control chart) of the process of processing the photograph of the Palmyra script. This diagram describes how the image processing operations, the data preparation procedure for deep neural network learning, and the final transcription (transliteration) of the script into digital form are performed.

4.6 YOLOv5 Instance Segmentation

Instance segmentation models are usually built on object detections models with alternations to predict polygonal labels. There are two types of detectors – one and two stage. The main difference between one-stage and two-stage detectors is the approach used to predict object locations and class labels. One-stage detectors make predictions in a single pass through the network, while two-stage detectors first generate region proposals and then classify objects within those regions. One-stage detectors are faster but less accurate, while two-stage detectors are more accurate but slower. The choice of which detector to use depends on the specific application requirements, including speed and accuracy. As we wanted our solution to work on mobile phones as well, we opted for a single-stage detector edited for instance-segmentation. Therefore, our selected algorithm for instance segmentation was YOLOv5 [29], which was released in 2020 as an object detector and in 2022 extended to instance segmentation.

During training YOLOv5 instance segmentation model, we minimize the three following losses. YOLO also minimizes classification loss, but since we only have one class, we do not track it in this research.

- box loss – it calculates how well the algorithm finds the center of the object and how well the bounding boxes overlap the object.
- seg loss – segmentation loss, it calculates, how well the algorithm creates segmentation masks, how much they fit into the actual shape of the target object.
- obj loss – objectness loss, it is the algorithm's confidence that an object exists within a given box (apart from polygons, yolo also predicts boxes).

In contrast, we maximize the metric mAP (= mean average precision).

5 Results

5.1 Dataset

We have labelled 28 images of Palmyrene inscriptions so far, with 1343 Palmyrene characters. 24 images were put in training, 1 image to validation and 2 images to testing subsets. We have selected several augmentation methods in Roboflow:

- Grayscale: Apply to 100% of images
- Saturation: Between −82% and + 82%
- Brightness: Between −20% and + 20%
- Exposure: Between −10% and + 10%
- Noise: Up to 5% of pixels

By using this augmentation, the final dataset contained 75 images in total. The dataset is available at [30].

5.2 SW Development Model

In the following three figures, we show the corresponding BPNM and flow diagrams. Figures 4 and 5 include one diagram split in half due to its size (Fig. 3).

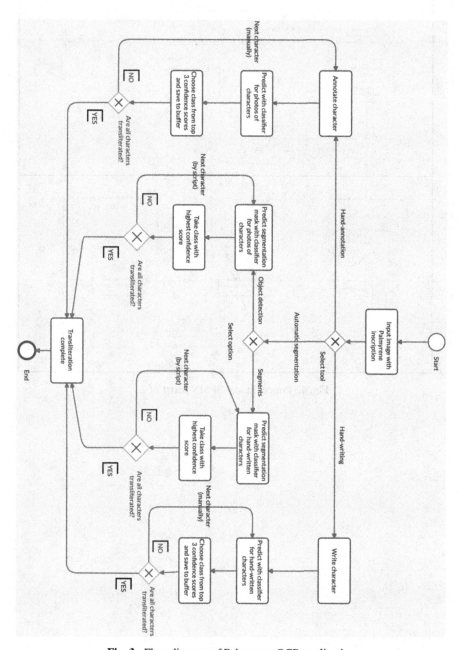

Fig. 3. Flow diagram of Palmyrene OCR application

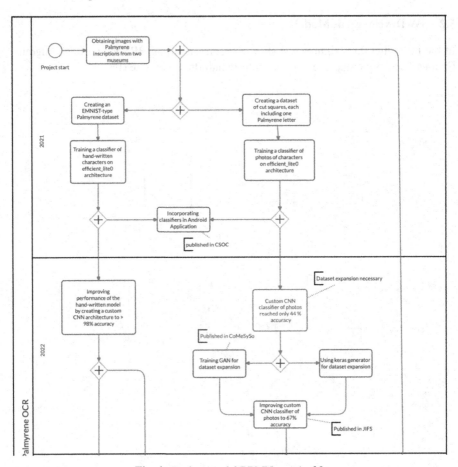

Fig. 4. Project model BPMN part 1 of 2

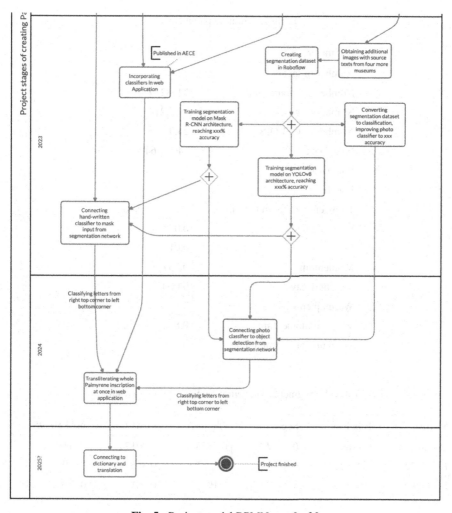

Fig. 5. Project model BPMN part 2 of 2

5.3 YOLOv5 Instance Segmentation

We have trained a YOLOv5 instance segmentation model with the following parameters on Google Colaboratory using GPU engine (Table 1).

At the start and at the end of training, the tracked metrics showed following values. First three epochs were warm-up epochs, so the metrics are tracked from epoch 4 (Table 2).

Table 1. Training parameters

Parameter	Value
Number of layers	225
Number of parameters	7408214
Number of gradients	7408214
Number of GFLOPs	24.9
Image size	640 × 640
Batch size	16
Epochs	100
Transfer learning initial model	Yolov5s-seg.pt
Learning rate	0.01
Lrf	0.01
Momentum	0.937
Weight decay	0.0005
Warmup epochs	3
Warmup momentum	0.8
Warmup bias learning rate	0.1

Table 2. Segmentation neural network training progress

Metrics	Box loss	Seg loss	Obj loss	mAP50	mAP50–95
Epoch 4	0.1164	0.1007	0.2553	0.00174	0.000174
Epoch 52	0.06822	0.04918	0.2365	0.815	0.305
Epoch 99	0.04529	0.04586	0.19	0.881	0.368

The images in the validation subset reached the following prediction result. We have removed displaying bounding boxes and confidence scores by editing utils/plots.py in yolo (Fig. 6):

Fig. 6. Prediction using YOLOv5 segmentation network.

5.4 Prediction Using Draw-Polygon Tool and Custom Classifier

The draw-polygon tool being developed is currently capable of drawing polygonal labels onto empty images and saving them without taking the order of letters into consideration. This could be useful for demonstration purposes, however, there are still some steps that need to be taken in order for the tool to become fully usable. The tool is still in an early stage of development and requires further refinement, testing, and debugging before it can be used in practical application.

6   Discussion

6.1   Comments on Results

We have presented a work-in-progress solution of Palmyrene OCR. The results provided consist of a YOLOv5 instance segmentation model, which was trained to recognize Palmyrene inscriptions using 28 labelled images with 1343 characters. The model was trained with a variety of augmentation methods to increase the size of the dataset and improve its robustness. The results show that after 100 epochs, the model achieved good performance, with an mAP50 of 0.881. Additionally, the draw-polygon tool is being developed to allow for the drawing of polygonal labels onto empty images. The excellent mAP score suggests that it is possible to create reliable segmentation masks and thus identify the Palmyrene characters correctly. The presented development diagram shows which steps were taken to reach these results and which steps still remain and the second diagram shows what options are and will be available in our application.

6.2 Comparison with Other Authors' Works

There was multiple related research, which we can compare our results with. Among them are some sources already mentioned in the literature overview as well as some more. The field of OCR has seen significant developments in recent years, and researchers are continuously working towards improving the accuracy and efficiency of OCR systems. In this discussion, we can see the results of several OCR projects, each targeting a different aspect of the problem.

Sayeed et al. [11] propose a low-cost novel convolutional neural network architecture for the recognition of Bengali characters. The authors have considered 8 different formations of CMATERdb datasets based on previous studies for the training phase and have shown that their proposed system outperformed previous works by a noteworthy margin for all 8 datasets. Moreover, they have tested their trained models on other available Bengali characters datasets and achieved 96–99% overall accuracies.

Ghosh et al. [10] focuses on the recognition of 231 different Bangla handwritten characters using state-of-the-art pre-trained CNN architectures. The authors have shown that InceptionResNetV2 achieved the best accuracy (96.99%) after 50 epochs, while DenseNet121 and InceptionNetV3 also provided remarkable recognition accuracy (96.55 and 96.20%, respectively). The authors have also considered the combination of trained InceptionResNetV2, InceptionNetV3, and DenseNet121 architectures, which provided better recognition accuracy (97.69%) than other single CNN architectures. However, it is not feasible for using as it requires a lot of computation power and memory. The authors have tested the models in the cases where characters look confusing to humans, and all the architectures showed equal capability in recognizing these images.

Doush et al.'s project [9] proposed an Arabic printed OCR dataset, extracted randomly from Wikipedia, with 4,587 Arabic articles and a total of 8,994 images. This dataset is expected to be a valuable resource for the research community to build robust Arabic OCR systems.

Nashwan et al. [31] introduced a computationally efficient, holistic Arabic OCR system, using a lexicon reduction approach based on clustering similar shaped words to reduce recognition time. The system managed to generalize for new font sizes that were not included in the training data, and the evaluation results were promising compared with state-of-the-art Arabic OCR systems.

Radwan et al. [32] presented an open vocabulary Arabic text recognition system using two neural networks, one for segmentation and another one for characters recognition. The segmentation model showed high accuracy of 98.9% for one font and 95.5% for four fonts, while the character recognition accuracy was 94.8% for Arabic Transparent font of size 18 pt from APTI dataset.

Amara et al. [33] is discussing the importance of OCR in various applications and the challenges in segmenting Arabic characters for OCR. To prevent segmentation errors, the authors propose a binary support vector machine (SVM) to decide whether to affirm segmentation points or re-do the segmentation, and deep learning methods to classify the characters.

Hussain et al. [34] presented a new approach for segmentation-based analysis for Nastalique style of Urdu language OCR. The segmentation-based method was optimized using 79,093 instances of 5249 main bodies, giving recognition accuracy of 97.11%. The system was then tested on document images of books with 87.44% main body recognition accuracy.

From this comparison, we can see, that our dataset is very small in comparison to other author's works. By annotating more images and by this, using more instances of Palmyrene characters for the training, we could reach over 90% accuracy in our recognition if we use more data for training our segmentation algorithm. We have already reached 88% with limited dataset size, so the potential is very promising.

6.3 Next Steps

Based on the results comparison, in later phases of this research, we will annotate more images of Palmyrene inscriptions. We also need to improve the draw-polygon tool by taking original image size into consideration and before drawing the polygons, first sorting the segments in left-to-right top-to-bottom order, as Palmyrene Aramaic is read this way, and then classify the polygons (characters) in the selected order with our previously developed classifier [14]. During the classification, each of these images will be assigned to a category of 28 Palmyrene characters and written down as Latin transliteration in the right order. The plans are also to implement this feature in the web and mobile applications.

The final step of creating a complete Palmyrene OCR is to create a Palmyrene NLP algorithm with a dictionary for translations to other languages, with the help of historians capable of translating Palmyrene Aramaic. We believe that our system can significantly improve the awareness of Palmyrene history to the general public, as well as speed up text recognition of newly discovered Palmyrene texts by researchers.

7 Conclusion

We have created a segmentation dataset of Palmyrene alphabet, which has several scientific contributions, namely increasing preservation and accessibility of Palmyrene artifacts and creating a cornerstone for the Palmyrene OCR system. As Palmyrene inscriptions are a valuable source of information about the culture, history, and language of ancient Palmyra, by creating a segmentation dataset of these inscriptions, we can make them more accessible to a wider audience, including scholars, students, and the general public.

Acknowledgment. This article was created with the support of the Internal Grant Agency (IGA) Faculty of Management and Economy, Czech University of Life Sciences in Prague, 2023A0004 – "Text segmentation methods for historical alphabets in the development of OCR".

References

1. Hammer, M.M., Champy, J.A.: Reengineering the Corporation: A Manifesto for Business Revolution. HarperBusiness Essentials, New York (2003). ISBN 978-0060559533
2. Pavlicek, J., Hronza, R., Pavlickova, P., Jelinkova, K.: The business process model quality metrics. In: Pergl, R., Lock, R., Babkin, E., Molhanec, M. (eds.) Enterprise and Organizational Modeling and Simulation, EOMAS 2017. LNBIP, vol. 298, pp. 134–148. Springer, Cham. https://doi.org/10.1007/978-3-319-68185-6_10
3. Chaudhuri, A., Krupa M., Pratixa B., Soumya G.K.: Optical Character Recognition Systems for Different Languages with Soft Computing. Studies in Fuzziness and Soft Computing. Springer, Cham (2017). ISBN 978-3-319-50251-9. https://doi.org/10.1007/978-3-319-502 52-6
4. Arica, N., Yarman-Vural, F.T.: An overview of character recognition focused on off-line handwriting. IEEE Trans. Syst. Man Cybern. Part C (Appl. Rev.) 31(2), 216–233 (2001). ISSN 1094-6977. https://doi.org/10.1109/5326.941845
5. Yu, F.T.S., Jutamulia, S.: Optical Pattern Recognition. Cambridge University Press, New York (1998). ISBN 978-0521465175
6. Gordin, S., et al.: Reading Akkadian cuneiform using natural language processing. PLOS ONE 15(10), e0240511 (2020). ISSN 1932-6203. https://doi.org/10.1371/journal.pone.024 0511
7. Hamplová, A., Franc, D., Pavlíček, J., Romach, A., Gordin, S.: Cuneiform reading using computer vision algorithms. In: 2022 5th International Conference on Signal Processing and Machine Learning, New York, pp. 242–245 (2022). ISBN 978-1-4503-9691-2. https://doi. org/10.1145/3556384.3556421
8. Alghamdi, M.A., Alhazi, I.S., Teahan, W.J.: Arabic OCR evaluation tool. In: 2016 7th International Conference on Computer Science and Information Technology (CSIT), pp. 1–6. IEEE (2016). ISBN 978-1-4673-8914-3. https://doi.org/10.1109/CSIT.2016.7549460
9. Doush, I.A., Aikhateeb, F., Gharibeh, A.H.: Yarmouk Arabic OCR dataset. In: 2018 8th International Conference on Computer Science and Information Technology (CSIT), pp. 150–154. IEEE (2018). ISBN 978-1-5386-4152-1. https://doi.org/10.1109/CSIT.2018.8486162
10. Ghosh, T., et al.: Bangla handwritten character recognition using MobileNet V1 architecture. Bull. Electr. Eng. Inform. 9(6), 2547–2554 (2020). ISSN 2302-9285. https://doi.org/10.11591/ eei.v9i6.2234
11. Sayeed, A., Shin, J., Hasan, M.A.M., Srizon, A.Y., Hasan, M.M.: BengaliNet: a low-cost novel convolutional neural network for Bengali handwritten characters recognition. Appl. Sci. 11(15), 242–245 (2021). ISBN 9781450396912. ISSN 2076-3417. https://doi.org/10. 3390/app11156845
12. Hajihashemi V., Ameri, M.M.A., Gharahbagh, A.A., Bastanfard, A.: A pattern recognition based Holographic Graph Neuron for Persian alphabet recognition. In: 2020 International Conference on Machine Vision and Image Processing (MVIP), pp. 1–6 (2020). https://doi. org/10.1109/MVIP49855.2020.9116913
13. Hamplová, A., Franc, D., Tyrychtr, J.: Historical alphabet transliteration software using computer vision classification approach. In: Silhavy, R. (ed.) Artificial Intelligence Trends in Systems, CSOC 2022. LNNS, pp. 34–45. Springer, Cham (2022). ISBN 978-3-031-09075-2. https://doi.org/10.1007/978-3-031-09076-9_4
14. Hamplová, A., Franc, D., Veselý, A.: An improved classifier and transliterator of hand-written Palmyrene letters to Latin. Neural Netw. World 32(4), 181–195 (2022). ISSN 23364335. https://doi.org/10.14311/NNW.2022.32.011
15. Franc, D., Hamplová, A., Svojše, O.: Augmenting historical alphabet datasets using generative adversarial networks. In: Silhavy, R., Silhavy, P., Prokopova, Z. (eds.) Data Science and

Algorithms in Systems, CoMeSySo 2022. LNNS, vol. 597, pp. 132–141. Springer, Cham (2023). ISBN 978-3-031-21437-0. https://doi.org/10.1007/978-3-031-21438-7_11

16. Kboubi, F., et al.: A new strategy of OCR combination. In: 8th World Multi-Conference on Systemics, Cybernetics and Informatics (SCI 2004), vol XII, Proceedings - Applications of Cybernetics and Informatics in Optics, Signals, Science and Engineering (2004)

17. Alghyaline, S.: Arabic optical character recognition: a review. CMES-Comput. Model. Eng. Sci. **135**(3), 1825–1861 (2023). ISSN 1526-1506. https://doi.org/10.32604/cmes.2022.024555

18. Natarajan, P.S., MacRostie, E., Decerbo, M.: The BBN Byblos Hindi OCR system. In: Proceedings of SPIE - The International Society for Optical Engineering: Document Recognition and Retrieval XII, pp. 10–16 (2005). https://doi.org/10.1117/12.588810

19. Kokawa, A., Busagala, L.S.P., Ohyama, W., Wakabayashi, T., Kimura, F.: An impact of OCR errors on automated classification of OCR Japanese texts with parts-of-speech analysis. In: 2011 International Conference on Document Analysis and Recognition, pp. 543–547. IEEE (2011). ISBN 978-1-4577-1350-7. https://doi.org/10.1109/ICDAR.2011.115

20. Nguyen, T.T.H., et al.: Deep statistical analysis of OCR errors for effective post-OCR processing. In: ACM-IEEE Joint Conference on Digital Libraries (JCDL), pp. 29–38 (2019). https://doi.org/10.1109/JCDL.2019.00015

21. Jain, P., Taneja, K., Taneja, H.: Which OCR toolset is good and why: a comparative study. Kuwait J. Sci. (KJS) **48**(2), 1–12 (2021). ISSN 2307-4116. https://doi.org/10.48129/kjs.v48i2.9589

22. Site officiel du Musée du Louvre. Le Louvre. (n.d.). http://www.louvre.fr

23. Al-As^{c}ad, K.: Aramaic Inscriptions in the Palmyra Museum. https://journals.openedition.org/syria/1478

24. Collection | Palmyra Archaeological Museum. https://virtual-museum-syria.org/palmyra/collection/

25. Palmyra | British Museum. https://www.britishmuseum.org/collection/search?keyword=Palmyra

26. ROM Online Collection - Royal Ontario Museum. https://collections.rom.on.ca/search/PALMYRA#filters

27. Roboflow: Give your software the power to see objects. https://www.roboflow.com

28. Cardanit: BPM software | Business Process and Decision. https://www.cardanit.com/

29. Jocher, G., et al.: ultralytics/yolov5. https://doi.org/10.5281/zenodo.5563715

30. Hamplová, A.: Instance segmentation dataset of Palmyrene characters, ZIP archive. https://app.roboflow.com/ds/6uKAAUoxOr?key=qch61mMNLp

31. Nashwan, F., Rashwan, M., Al-Barhamtoshy, H., Abdou, S., Moussa, A.: A Holistic technique for an Arabic OCR system. J. Imaging **4**(1), 6 (2018). ISSN 2313-433X. https://doi.org/10.3390/jimaging4010006

32. Radwan, M.A., Khalil, M.I., Abbas, H.M.: Predictive segmentation using multichannel neural networks in Arabic OCR system. In: Schwenker, F., Abbas, H., El Gayar, N., Trentin, E. (eds.) Artificial Neural Networks in Pattern Recognition. LNCS, vol. 9896, pp. 233–245. Springer, Cham (2016). ISBN 978-3-319-46181-6. https://doi.org/10.1007/978-3-319-46182-3_20

33. Amara, M., Zidi, K., Zidi, S., Ghedira, K.: Arabic character recognition based M-SVM: review. In: Hassanien, A.E., Tolba, M.F., Taher Azar, A., (eds.) Advanced Machine Learning Technologies and Applications. Communications in Computer and Information Science, vol. 488, pp. 18–25. Springer, Cham (2014). ISBN 978-3-319-13460-4. https://doi.org/10.1007/978-3-319-13461-1_3

34. Hussain, S., Ali, S., Akram, Q.u.A.: Nastalique segmentation-based approach for Urdu OCR. Int. J. Doc. Anal. Recogn. (IJDAR) **18**(4), 357–374 (2015). ISSN 1433-2833. https://doi.org/10.1007/s10032-015-0250-2

On the Relevance of Explanation for RDF Resources Similarity

Simona Colucci[1(✉)], Francesco M. Donini[2], and Eugenio Di Sciascio[1]

[1] Politecnico di Bari, Bari, Italy
{simona.colucci,eugenio.disciascio}@poliba.it
[2] Università degli Studi della Tuscia, Viterbo, Italy
donini@unitus.it

Abstract. Artificial Intelligence (AI) has been shown to productively affect organizational decision making, in terms of returned economic value. In particular, agile business may significantly benefit from the ability of AI systems to constantly pursue contextual knowledge awareness. Undoubtedly, a key added value of such systems is the ability to explain results. In fact, users are more inclined to trust and feel the accountability of systems, when the output is returned together with a human-readable explanation. Nevertheless, some of the information in an explanation might be *irrelevant* to users—despite its truthfulness. This paper discusses the relevance of explanation for resources similarity, provided by AI systems. In particular, the analysis focuses on one system based on Large Language Models (LLMs)—namely ChatGPT— and on one logic-based tool relying on the computation of the Least Common Subsumer in the Resource Description Framework (RDF). This discussion reveals the need for a formal distinction between relevant and irrelevant information, that we try to answer with a definition of relevance amenable to implementation.

Keywords: Explainable Artificial Intelligence (XAI) · Explanation Relevance · Large Language Models (LLMs) · Resource Description Framework (RDF) · Least Common Subsumer (LCS)

1 Introduction

The role of Artificial intelligence (AI) in providing business value is nowadays universally recognized and has been widely investigated [10]. In particular, it has been discussed the opportunity of embedding AI techniques in processes traditionally performed by humans—like strategical and organizational decision making [24], recruitment [23], and corporate training [7]. A key feature of AI systems is their ability to constantly acquire new knowledge from the context, either by learning or by reasoning on formal models. This ability is crucial in supporting business organizations to rapidly adapt to changing conditions, or, in other words, to pursue *agility*.

© The Author(s), under exclusive license to Springer Nature Switzerland AG 2023
E. Babkin et al. (Eds.): MOBA 2023, LNBIP 488, pp. 96–107, 2023.
https://doi.org/10.1007/978-3-031-45010-5_8

The observations above motivate the investigation on a model of governance for businesses based on AI [19]. The work by Schneider *et al.* [19] also collects main open challenges in this kind of governance. Among them, the authors refer to two undesirable features of AI output: i) it is often not understandable; ii) some results are beyond the control of an organization.

In fact, the ability of AI systems to provide their users an explanation for a given behavior is nowadays considered as an important feature [17], improving, among others, trustworthiness and accountability of the system. In particular, a *logic-based* approach has been advocated [12] to compute and validate explanations [9]. However, methodologies for computing explanations usually do not consider the user whom the explanation is given to—in Miller's words [17, p.29], "an explanation is an interaction between two roles: explainer and explainee". In this respect, the various parts an explanation can be made of should be *relevant* for the user—not just trivially true—what Miller summarizes as *epistemic relevance* in explanations [17, p.38].

In the realm of logic-based explanations, in this paper we focus on relevance in explaining similarity of RDF resources, *i.e.*, logical methods for constructing (relevant) explanations about why two or more RDF resources were declared similar—or equivalently, why they were put in the same cluster. In a recent paper [5], Colucci *et al.* explored the verbalization of logical explanations regarding why some tenders in a Public Procurement knowledge graph were clustered by standard algorithms, like k-Means. Colucci *et al.* made use of Least Common Subsumers (LCS) [4] of RDF resources to verbalize an explanation of the similarities among them. However, in the examples presented, pertinent phrases were mixed with general information. For instance [5, Fig. 2], all recorded tenders were completed, so reporting the information of a "status complete", or the information that all tenders referred to a classification schema called "Common Procurement Vocabulary (CPV)", while being true, was not epistemically relevant. In contrast, the information that all tenders in the cluster referred to truck transportation was relevant in the general context of tenders.

The problem is that all information present in an LCS of a set of resources S is "relevant" in the usual sense, in that it describes some characteristic which truly belongs to each single resource. However, the epistemically relevant information should be one that

1. *discriminates* resources in S with respect to other resources not in S (what has been also called *contrastive* explanation in other contexts), and
2. is *not already known* by the user—which appeals to the fact that the explanatory service should maintain a *model* of the user being informed.

In the following sections, we analyze some answers of the system by Colucci *et al.* , pointing out the irrelevant parts of the explanations it gives. We analyze also a state-of-the-art Large Language Model (LLM), namely ChatGPT, and find that LLMs too fail to make a distinction between relevant and irrelevant information in explaining the similarity of some items. To overcome such limitations, in Sect. 4 we attempt a logical definition of relevance addressing Points 1–2 above, which may lead us—in future research—to mechanize the computation of relevant explanations for similarity and clusterization. A final section concludes the paper.

2   Comparing LCS with LLM

LLMs have recently reached an indisputable fame and become rather pervasive in real life, mostly thanks to the public availability of ChatGPT[1], a chatbot providing detailed and articulate answers to questions across different knowledge domains. In a nutshell, the term LLM denotes deep learning models with a couple of distinguishing characteristics: *(i)* their number of parameters is at least in the order of billions; *(ii)* they are general-purpose systems, trained for excellently performing a wide set of tasks.

ChatGPT implements as a Web API the Generative Pre-trained Transformer 3.5 (GPT-3.5) [3], a LLM developed by OpenAI to produce natural language text on the basis of deep learning techniques [18]. The answers returned by ChatGPT are quite impressive in terms of information richness and readability, as every user may verify by querying the chatbot.

As an example, by asking "What do the drugs "cefepime" and "ceftazidime" have in common?", ChatGPT[2] returns the explanation below:

Cefepime and ceftazidime are both cephalosporin antibiotics, which means they belong to a class of medications that are used to treat bacterial infections. They both work by inhibiting the synthesis of the bacterial cell wall, which leads to the death of the bacteria and the resolution of the infection. Cefepime and ceftazidime are similar in that they both have a broad spectrum of activity and can be used to treat a wide range of infections caused by different types of bacteria. They are both active against many gram-positive and gram-negative bacteria, including some species of Pseudomonas and Escherichia coli. However, cefepime and ceftazidime differ in some respects. Cefepime has a more extended spectrum of activity than ceftazidime, meaning it is effective against a wider range of bacteria. Cefepime is also more resistant to certain types of beta-lactamases, enzymes produced by bacteria that can break down cephalosporin antibiotics and make them less effective. Ceftazidime is more often used to treat infections in the respiratory tract, urinary tract, and skin, while cefepime is more often used to treat infections in the blood and urinary tract.

This answer is learned by facts collected in the Web from published documents.

Nevertheless, knowledge is not always available in such a plain format: Linked Open Data (LOD) [20] also represents a valuable information source for answering users questions. In this context, knowledge is available in RDF syntax [11] and usually publicly accessible.

---

[1] https://chat.openai.com/.
[2] Queried on December, 28th 2022.

```
1)They are all Organic Chemical that is Chemical Viewed Structurally ;
2)They are all Antibiotic that is Pharmacologic Substance
3)They are all C preparations that is Classification
4)They are all C preparations that is Drug Products by Generic Ingredient Combinations
5)They all has_ingredient something that is Organic Chemical that is Chemical Viewed Structurally ;
6)They all has_ingredient something that is Antibiotic that is Pharmacologic Substance ;
7)They all has_physiologic_effect Decreased Cell Wall Synthesis & Repair that is Organ or Tissue Function ;
8)They all has_physiologic_effect Decreased Cell Wall Synthesis & Repair that is Cell Wall Alteration;
9)They all may_treat Serratia Infections that is Enterobacteriaceae Infections;
10)They all may_treat something that is Enterobacteriaceae Infections;
11)They all may_treat Urinary Tract Infections  that is Infection;
12)They all may_treat something that is Infection;
13)They all may_treat Acinetobacter Infections  that is Moraxellaceae Infections ;
14)They all may_treat Escherichia coli Infections that is Enterobacteriaceae Infections  ;
15)They all may_treat something that is Enterobacteriaceae Infections;
16)They all may_treat Neutropenia  that is Agranulocytosi;
17)They all may_treat Pneumonia, Bacterial that is Bacterial Infections ;
18)They all may_treat something that is Bacterial Infections ;
19)They all may_treat Haemophilus Infections  that is Pasteurellaceae Infections  ;
20)They all may_treat Streptococcal Infections  that is Gram-Positive Bacterial Infections  ;
21)They all may_treat something that is Gram-Positive Bacterial Infections  ;
22)They all may_treat Proteus Infections  that is Enterobacteriaceae Infection;
23)They all may_treat Fever that is Finding ;
24)They all may_treat Fever that is Body Temperature Changes ;
25)They all may_treat Fever induced_by PLAGUE VACCINE INJ  ;
26)They all may_treat Sepsis  that is Infection ;
27)They all may_treat Pseudomonas Infections  that is Gram-Negative Bacterial Infections ;
28)They all may_treat Klebsiella Infections  that is Enterobacteriaceae Infections  ;
29)They all may_treat Bone Diseases, Infectious  that is Bone Diseases ;
30)They all may_treat Skin Diseases, Bacterial that is Bacterial Infections;
31)They all are contraindicated with Drug Hypersensitivity  that is Hypersensitivity  ;
32)They all has_mechanism_of_action Enzyme Inhibitors that is Molecular Function ;
33)They all share has_mechanism_of_action Enzyme Inhibitors  that is Enzyme Interactions  ;
```

Fig. 1. Explanation of the commonalities between "cefepime" (http://purl.bioontology. org/ontology/NDFRT/N0000022054) and "ceftazidime" (http://purl.bioontology.org/ ontology/NDFRT/N0000145931) computed through an independent implementation of the verbalization tool by Colucci et al. [5]

As an example, we extracted from Bioportal[3] the explanation in Fig. 1 for the similarity of the same two resources (through an independent implementation of the verbalization tool by Colucci et al. [5]).

The reader may notice that the returned answer is less human-readable than the one from ChatGPT, but rather detailed and informative.

Unfortunately, if we query ChatGPT about knowledge available *only* on the Web of Data, returned answers look like not exploiting RDF knowledge content.

For instance, TheyBuyForYou (TBFY) knowledge graph [21] includes an ontology for procurement data, based on the Open Contracting Data Standard (OCDS) [22]. Figure 2 shows the answer by ChatGPT, when asked for comparing two referenced contracting processes:

http://data.tbfy.eu/contractingProcess/ocds-0c46vo-0133-026258-2019 and

http://data.tbfy.eu/contractingProcess/ocds-0c46vo-0001-76e76119-992d-40ef-8444-7b020809ff81 .

By carefully inspecting the answer in Fig. 2, the reader may notice that only generic information about the knowledge graph structure is returned. The chatbot ends up to admit the hardness of providing an explanation for similarity.

Yet, the verbalization tool by Colucci et al. [5] is able to provide the explanation in Fig. 3 for the similarity of the same two referenced contracting processes, by exploiting only the knowledge in TBFY.

---

[3] https://bioportal.bioontology.org/.

explain similarity of "http://data.tbfy.eu/contractingProcess/ocds-0c46vo-0001-76e76119-992d-40ef-8444-7b020809ff81" and "http://data.tbfy.eu/contractingProcess/ocds-0c46vo-0133-026258-2019"

The URLs "http://data.tbfy.eu/contractingProcess/ocds-0c46vo-0001-76e76119-992d-40ef-8444-7b020809ff81" and "http://data.tbfy.eu/contractingProcess/ocds-0c46vo-0133-026258-2019" are both links to procurement information on the TheyBuyForYou website. They both represent a specific procurement process and they are similar in that they both contain the same prefix "http://data.tbfy.eu/contractingProcess" which suggests that they are both part of the same dataset of public procurement information.

The similarities don't end there, they both contain the prefix "ocds-0c46vo" which is a standard format for Open Contracting Data Standard (OCDS) and it's used to identify procurement information. The rest of the string of characters in the URL are unique identifiers that are specific to each procurement.

It can be inferred that these two procurement processes are related in some way and they were released by the same organization, but without more information on the procurement it's hard to know more about the similarity.

Fig. 2. Chat, dated January 16, 2023, about the similarity of two referenced contracting processes in TBFY: http://data.tbfy.eu/contractingProcess/ocds-0c46vo-0133-026258-2019 and http://data.tbfy.eu/contractingProcess/ocds-0c46vo-0001-76e76119-992d-40ef-8444-7b020809ff81

```
The resources in analysis present the following properties in common:

1) They all have a release referencing some resource
        which  has publisher name "Open Opps"
        and  has publisher schema "Companies House"
        and  has publisher web page "https://openopps.com"

2) They all present a tender referencing some resource
        which   require a specific item(s) referencing some resource
        which  has classification code "34134000 (Flatbed and Tipper trucks)"
        and  has classification schema "Common Procurement Vocabulary (CPV)"

        and  has tender status "complete"
```

Fig. 3. Verbal explanation for the similarity of two referenced resources: http://data.tbfy.eu/contractingProcess/ocds-0c46vo-0133-026258-2019 and http://data.tbfy.eu/contractingProcess/ocds-0c46vo-0001-76e76119-992d-40ef-8444-7b020809ff81

The explanation in Fig. 3 is built on the computation of a Common Subsumer (CS) of the two contracting processes, as detailed in the work by Colucci *et al.* [5]. Figure 4 shows the CS knowledge graph, as an evidence of the existing commonalities between the two contracting processes.

The reader may agree on the greater informativeness of the explanation in Fig. 3 w.r.t. the one returned by ChatGPT in Fig. 2.

3 A Critical View on Relevance in Explanations

In the previous section, we showed by example that the informative richness of explanation services depends on the underlying knowledge model. In particular, when the domain is modelled in RDF, a LCS-based approach seems to be able to return richer explanations than ChatGPT. On the contrary, when knowledge is available in web documents, LLMs-based tools reach an impressive informative level.

By the way, none of the above-mentioned approaches copes with the problem of providing explanations which are *epistemically relevant* to the querying entity. Indeed, often explanations include obvious information, describing a common knowledge in the specific query domain.

To support our thesis, we refer to examples both in ChatGPT and in the verbalization tool by Colucci *et al.* [5]. Recalling Point 2 in the Introduction, the irrelevance of an explanation may depend on the knowledge of the user to be informed: the answer should provide information that the user does not already know.

First, we go back to ChatGPT answer to the question: "What do the drugs "cefepime" and "ceftazidime" have in common?". The first sentence in the response includes a definition for antibiotics (.....*antibiotics, which means they belong to a class of medications that are used to treat bacterial infections*) that, although true, is obvious in the medical domain and known by every physician. An explanation targeted to the medical field should omit such an information.

Also by looking at the explanation in Fig. 1, the reader may notice that at least lines 12 and 18 are completely irrelevant to physicians, as well as the second part of lines 24, that includes a definition for "fever".

Let us consider now the answer in Fig. 2; the second paragraph includes a reference to a common prefix:

... *they both contain the same prefix* "http://data.tbfy.eu/contractingProcess" *which suggests that they are both part of the same dataset of public procurement information.*

which is irrelevant to every user able to refer to specific TBFY URIs in the query. The answer to such a query could omit the information about common prefix without any informative loss.

For further examples, we apply the LCS-based verbalization tool to clustering results in TBFY. In particular, all contracting processes released on January, 30th 2019 have been clustered with K-means [13] algorithm[4] and the smallest cluster has been explained in terms of commonalities (on the basis of the LCS of all items in it).

The resulting explanation is given in Fig. 5.

---

[4] The implementation at https://scikit-learn.org/stable/modules/generated/sklearn. cluster.KMeans.html has been used.

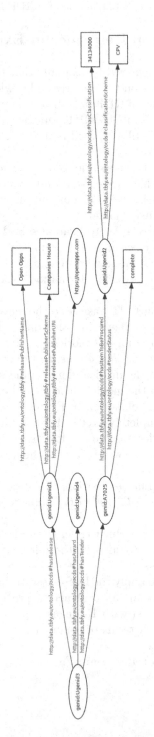

Fig. 4. A Common Subsumer (CS) of the two referenced resources: http://data. tbfy.eu/contractingProcess/ocds-0c46vo-0133-026258-2019 and http://data.tbfy.eu/ contractingProcess/ocds-0c46vo-0001-76e76119-992d-40ef-8444-7b020809ff81

The resources in analysis present the following properties in common:

```
1) They all have a release referencing some resource
        which  has publisher name "Open Opps"
        and  has publisher schema "Companies House"
        and  has release publisher "TICON UK LIMITED"
        and  has publisher web page "https://openopps.com"
        and  has release date "30 January 2019"
```

Fig. 5. Explanation (obtained by using the Common Subsumer technology) of the commonalities in the smallest cluster returned by clustering with k-Means all contracting processes released on January 30, 2019.

The last sentence in Fig. 5 states that all contracting process in the cluster have been released on January 30, 2019, which is a feature common to all items in the clustered dataset. This causes the information to be irrelevant to the audience. In other words, when we search for commonalities in a subset of resources, all features that are also common to larger sets should be not put in evidence in the explanation.

All observations above ask for a formal definition of explanation *relevance* in all its facets. Thus, we try to formalize the main aspects of such definitions in the next section.

4   Defining Relevance in CS-Based Explanations

There have been several attempts to define relevance in symbolic Artificial Intelligence [14,16]. However, such attempts concentrate on *relevance for reasoning*, a concept which is tightly coupled with independence [15]—a formula ψ is irrelevant for another formula ϕ if the interpretation of ϕ is independent from the interpretation of ψ. The concept of relevance was also studied in the Information Retrieval (IR) research field [2]. However, relevance in IR is about document relevance, as it aims "...to retrieve all the relevant documents [and] at the same time retrieving as few of the non-relevant as possible" [25, p.6]. This aim leads to definitions that may either involve a subjective judgement about the retrieval task and the user's needs [2], or a probabilistic analysis of relevance based on documents descriptions [26]. In both cases, we did not find connections to the concept of relevance in explaining similarity.

In our case, we are interested on the relevance of communicating *parts* of an LCS, when both the LCS itself, and the background knowledge about a user, are represented in RDF. To the best of out knowledge, definitions in the field of IR do not cope with RDF/RDFS; thus, we provide new, RDF-specific definitions for relevance. In our past research, we already dealt with problem of providing informative (L)CS [8], but w.r.t. Description Logics (DLs) [1].

We concentrate first on *relevance in a context*, meaning that some characteristics, that are in common to a given set of resources S, may not be relevant to communicate because they are common also to larger sets of resources $T \supset S$, while others do. We introduce this kind of relevance with an example based on the previous sections.

Example 1. 0 Suppose T is a set of resources representing all European contracting processes of a given day of the year, say, January 30, 2019, and $S = \{r_1, r_2\} \subset T$ is a pair of such resources that an algorithm like k-Means, while clustering T, puts in the same cluster. Clearly r_1 and r_2 share the same release date "2019-01-30"; however, *in the larger context of* T which these resources were drawn from, this information is irrelevant. If instead r_1 and r_2 were drawn from the set $T' \supset T$ of *all* tenders in the whole year 2019, being released in the same date would become relevant.

Intuitively, a common characteristic P of a set of resources S is relevant in the context of a larger set T, when P is *not* common to the larger set T. In the following, formal definition, we refer to the notion of LCS as defined by Colucci *et al.* [4].

Definition 1. *[Relevance w.r.t. a larger set] Let T, S be sets of RDF resources, with $S \subset T$, and for each resource $r \in T$, a rooted graph $\langle r, T \rangle$ can be computed. Let $L = \langle x, T \rangle$ the rooted graph representing the Least Common Subsumer of all resources in S, and let $P \subseteq L$ a path in L starting from x.*
We say that P is relevant in T if $LCS(T) \not\models P$.

The above definition of relevance may model *contrastive* explanations, in the following sense: given a resource r which has *not* been put into a cluster S of resources, a contrastive explanation about "Why resources in S were put in the same cluster, while r was not?" can be formed by taking the LCS of S, and the LCS of $T = S \cup \{r\}$, and finding a characteristic which is in the former but not in the latter.

A different notion of relevance comes up when user's knowledge—at least that part that can be expressed in RDF—can be taken into account. Again, we introduce this aspect with another example:

Example 2. When identifying the common characteristics of two antibiotics in a drugs databank [6], a common characteristics that is—correctly—found is that they both "are used in bacterial infections". This information may be useful for a generic user, while for a physician it would be trivially irrelevant. In this case, the knowledge that the system implicitly attributes to the user comes into play. The system should be able to distinguish at least between a generic user and a physician, and choose epistemically relevant information accordingly.

Intuitively, a characteristic P is relevant for a user u when it is not part of u's prior knowledge; a formal definition can be made as follows:

Definition 2. *[Relevance w.r.t. a user's knowledge] Let S be a set of RDF resources, and for each resource $r \in S$, a rooted graph $\langle r, S \rangle$ can be computed. Let $L = \langle x, S \rangle$ the rooted graph representing the Least Common Subsumer of all resources in S, and let $P \subseteq L$ a path in L starting from x. Moreover, let K_u*

be the RDF-graph representing the knowledge (espressible in RDF) of a given user u.

We say that P is relevant *for u if* $K_u \not\models P$.

Observe that it is not necessary to elicit K_u from the user through a long—and presumably tedious—knowledge elicitation process. As a first attempt, the system may use as K_u a domain ontology, whose knowledge can be commonly attributed to specific user categories, such as physicians or procurement brokers.

5 Conclusion

In this paper, we analyzed the explanations about the similarity of two or more resources, drawn from the Business domain of Public Procurement, and the biological domain of drugs. The compared explanations were given by the RDF-logic-based system of Colucci *et al.* [5] and the LLM-based system of ChatGPT. We highlighted that both approaches mix relevant and irrelevant information, where relevance can be evaluated based on *(i)* either a larger context of resources, *(ii)* or prior user's expert knowledge. Finally, for the case of knowledge expressed in RDF, we provided two objective, logical definitions of relevance of information in such explanations, one for each of the above characterizations of relevance.

Regarding future work, we plan to implement the definitions of relevance given in the previous section by adding an RDF Reasoner in the pipeline building the linguistic realization of the LCS. To exploit Definition 1, we plan to compute the LCS of a larger set of resources, and check for non-implication. In this way, our tool for providing explanations may avoid verbalizing trivial information about commonalities that are also common to supersets. Regarding Definition 2, we do not plan for the moment to try to model knowledge of single users—this would be too time-consuming. Instead, we plan to use RDF ontologies for specific domains, like those in Bioportal[5], which can model common knowledge of users expert of the domain.

Acknowledgements. Projects Regione Lazio-DTC/"SanLo" (CUP F85F21001-090003) and Ministero dello Sviluppo Ecnoncomico/"Casa delle Tecnologie Emergenti dell'area metropolitana di Bari: Bari Open Innovation Hub" (CUP J99J19000300003) partially supported this work.

References

1. Baader, F., Calvanese, D., McGuinness, D., Patel-Schneider, P., Nardi, D.: The Description Logic Handbook: Theory, Implementation and Applications. Cambridge University Press (2003)
2. Borlund, P.: The concept of relevance in IR. J. Am. Soc. Inf. Sci. Technol. **54**(10), 913–925 (2003). https://onlinelibrary.wiley.com/doi/abs/10.1002/asi.10286
3. Brown, T., et al.: Language models are few-shot learners. Adv. Neural. Inf. Process. Syst. **33**, 1877–1901 (2020)

---

[5] https://bioportal.bioontology.org/ontologies.

4. Colucci, S., Donini, F., Giannini, S., Di Sciascio, E.: Defining and computing least common subsumers in RDF. Web Semant. Sci. Serv. Agents World Wide Web **39**, 62–80 (2016)
5. Colucci, S., Donini, F.M., Iurilli, N., Di Sciascio, E.: A business intelligence tool for explaining similarity. In: Babkin, E., Barjis, J., Malyzhenkov, P., Merunka, V. (eds.) Model-Driven Organizational and Business Agility - Second International Workshop, MOBA 2022, Leuven, Belgium, 6–7 June 2022, Revised Selected Papers. Lecture Notes in Business Information Processing, vol. 457, pp. 50–64. Springer, Cham (2022). https://doi.org/10.1007/978-3-031-17728-6_5
6. Colucci, S., Donini, F.M., Di Sciascio, E.: Logical comparison over RDF resources in bio-informatics. J. Biomed. Informatics **76**, 87–101 (2017). https://doi.org/10.1016/j.jbi.2017.11.004
7. Colucci, S., Di Noia, T., Di Sciascio, E., Donini, F.M., Ragone, A.: Semantic-based skill management for automated task assignment and courseware composition. J. Univers. Comput. Sci. **13**(9), 1184–1212 (2007). https://doi.org/10.3217/jucs-013-09-1184
8. Colucci, S., Tinelli, E., Di Sciascio, E., Donini, F.M.: Automating competence management through non-standard reasoning. Eng. Appl. Artif. Intell. **24**(8), 1368–1384 (2011). https://doi.org/10.1016/j.engappai.2011.05.015
9. Cooper, M.C., Marques-Silva, J.: Tractability of explaining classifier decisions. Artif. Intell. **316**, 103841 (2023). https://www.sciencedirect.com/science/article/pii/S0004370222001813
10. Enholm, I.M., Papagiannidis, E., Mikalef, P., Krogstie, J.: Artificial intelligence and business value: a literature review. Inf. Syst. Front. **24**(5), 1709–1734 (2022)
11. Hayes, P., Patel-Schneider, P.F.: RDF 1.1 semantics, W3C recommendation (2014). https://www.w3.org/TR/2014/REC-rdf11-mt-20140225/
12. Ignatiev, A.: Towards trustable explainable AI. In: IJCAI, pp. 5154–5158 (2020)
13. Jin, X., Han, J.: K-Means Clustering, pp. 563–564. Springer, Boston (2010). https://doi.org/10.1007/978-0-387-30164-8_425
14. Lakemeyer, G.: Relevance from an epistemic perspective. Artif. Intell. **97**(1–2), 137–167 (1997). https://doi.org/10.1016/S0004-3702(97)00038-6
15. Lang, J., Liberatore, P., Marquis, P.: Propositional independence: formula-variable independence and forgetting. J. Artif. Intell. Res. **18**, 391–443 (2003). https://doi.org/10.1613/jair.1113
16. Levy, A.Y., Fikes, R., Sagiv, Y.: Speeding up inferences using relevance reasoning: a formalism and algorithms. Artif. Intell. **97**(1–2), 83–136 (1997). https://doi.org/10.1016/S0004-3702(97)00049-0
17. Miller, T.: Explanation in artificial intelligence: insights from the social sciences. Artif. Intell. **267**, 1–38 (2019). https://www.sciencedirect.com/science/article/pii/S0004370218305988
18. OpenAI: ChatGPT: optimizing language models for dialogue. https://web.archive.org/web/20221130180912/openai.com/blog/chatgpt/. Accessed 18 Apr 2023
19. Schneider, J., Abraham, R., Meske, C., Brocke, J.V.: Artificial intelligence governance for businesses. Inf. Syst. Manag. 1–21 (2022)
20. Shadbolt, N., Hall, W., Berners-Lee, T.: The semantic web revisited. Intell. Syst. IEEE **21**(3), 96–101 (2006)
21. Soylu, A., et al.: TheyBuyForYou platform and knowledge graph: expanding horizons in public procurement with open linked data. Semant. Web **13**(2), 265–291 (2022)

22. Soylu, A., et al.: Towards an ontology for public procurement based on the open contracting data standard. In: Pappas, I.O., et al. (eds.) I3E 2019. LNCS, vol. 11701, pp. 230–237. Springer, Cham (2019). https://doi.org/10.1007/978-3-030-29374-1_19

23. Tinelli, E., Cascone, A., Ruta, M., Di Noia, T., Di Sciascio, E., Donini, F.M.: I.M.P.A.K.T.: an innovative semantic-based skill management system exploiting standard SQL. In: Cordeiro, J., Filipe, J. (eds.) ICEIS 2009 - Proceedings of the 11th International Conference on Enterprise Information Systems, Volume AIDSS, Milan, Italy, 6–10 May 2009, pp. 224–229 (2009)

24. Trunk, A., Birkel, H., Hartmann, E.: On the current state of combining human and artificial intelligence for strategic organizational decision making. Bus. Res. **13**(3), 875–919 (2020)

25. Van Rijsbergen, C.: Information Retrieval (2nd edn). Butterworth-Heinemann, Newton (1979)

26. Van Rijsbergen, C.: Information retrieval: theory and practice. In: Proceedings of the joint IBM/University of Newcastle Upon Tyne Seminar on Data Base Systems, vol. 79 (1979)

Transformation of Class Hierarchies During Agile Software Development in UML

Vojtěch Merunka[1,2](✉), Himesha Wijekoon[1], and Boris Schegolev[1]

[1] Department of Information Engineering, Faculty of Economics and Management,
Czech University of Life Sciences Prague, Prague, Czech Republic
{merunka,wijekoon,schegolev}@pef.czu.cz,
vojtech.merunka@fjfi.cvut.cz
[2] Department of Software Engineering, Faculty of Nuclear Sciences and Engineering,
Czech Technical University in Prague, Prague, Czech Republic

Abstract. This article discusses support for the UML standard in the Agile software development. There are described some of the weaknesses of the UML standard that software developers should know about to take full advantage of this otherwise very good and desirable standard. Specifically, it is a hierarchy of object classes, which belongs to the basic concepts of the object-oriented paradigm. This hierarchy is considered well known, but in fact there are three slightly different hierarchies that fortunately fit well with the MDA philosophy. The problem is mainly that all these three hierarchies appear in UML in the same way, as if they were just one type of hierarchy. The article describes and explains these differences and suggests a refinement to the UML using stereotypes. The conclusions written in this article are a summary of the authors' experience of agile software projects having reduced formal documentation for the international consulting company Deloitte, Czech system integrator of telecommunications applications Datalite Ltd. and of university research and education.

Keywords: UML · software development life cycle · transformation of concepts · MDA · class hierarchies

1 Introduction

The objective of Unified Modelling Language (UML) has been and is to replace older methodologies of the aforesaid authors with one methodology that is a combination of the best of the older ones. Likewise, the Model Driven Architecture (MDA) philosophy is a synthesis of previous best experiences in the creation of large-scale software, where there is a semantic gap between programmers and people in the modeled problem.

The history of software engineering could be simply described as a human struggle with complexity. The solution is to split a complex task into a set of many smaller and therefore simpler tasks that one can already manage. Incidentally, this idea, which is the basis, for example, the programming of computers is not new. It was probably first pronounced by a Persian scientist Muhammad ibn Musa al-Khwarizmi in his book The

E. Babkin et al. (Eds.): MOBA 2023, LNBIP 488, pp. 108–117, 2023.
https://doi.org/10.1007/978-3-031-45010-5_9

Compendious Book on Calculation by Completion and Balancing which became the basis of modern mathematics and actually was the forerunner of software engineering [1, 2].

This paper is organized as follows:

- The introduction is followed by Sect. 2 on UML and its problems.
- This is followed by Sect. 3 on the MDA approach.
- Section 4 is central because it contains our own research which is described in a concrete example.
- Section 5 is a discussion and suggested solution.
- The conclusion of this article.

2 Object-Oriented Approach and the Origin of UML

Before the arrival of UML, in early 1990s, we had several competing object-oriented methodologies with mutually different notations. These were so called first genera-tion object-oriented methodologies. Many software companies used a combination of several methodologies instead of just one methodology – mostly object models from Object Modelling Technique (OMT) along with interaction diagrams from the Booch method and the Use-Case approach of the Jacobson Object-Oriented Software Engi-neering (OOSE) method [3–5]. Most of these methodologies have later become the foundation for UML [6]. UML has brought along a unification of the previous notations. The UML notation is mostly based on OMT and has become a recognized standard. UML includes many different elements from the original methodologies. There is, for example, the so called "business extension" from the original Jacobson method that has been added in version 1.x, or the absorption of the Specification and Description Language (SDL) methodology for supporting real-time processes in version 2.x [7].

Obviously, the UML is not a method. UML is "only" a modelling language [8]. That, itself should not be a problem – it is good that since 1996 we have had a standard for object modeling. The problem, however, is the fact that for the "universal" language there are more methodologies (e.g., Rational Unified Process) and even mere knowledge of UML is often considered a methodology [9].

2.1 Is UML a Method?

Experience proves that it is not. UML is not a method that could be understood by a layperson in reasonable time (for instance in 15 min at the beginning of a meeting with analysts) to be able to read and understand the diagrams. This is not an unrealistic requirement because in the past it was possible to work like this with entity-relational and data-flow models. Unfortunately, in object-oriented modeling we do not have such an elegant and simple method. Instead, we send customers to attend long training sessions on UML, where we make them work with CASE[1] tools.

---

[1] Computer Aided Software Engineering.

2.2 Some of the UML Issues

Most criticism at UML is directed at its complexity and inconsistency. It is, for example, the direction of the arrows of different links that sometimes draws in reverse with reality. Another criticism is the varying level of detail. For example, terms directly related to C++ or Java and similar programming languages have beautiful distinguishable symbols, but concepts also very important but not supported in Java-like programming languages have very little support or only optional textual stereotype. The third and last part of the criticism speaks of complicated or even no UML support for the decomposition and generalization of diagrams that no longer have the elegance of the old Data Flow Diagram (DFD). A good publication on this topic is an article by Simons and Graham [10].

However, we know many of these things also from other areas of science. As a typical example, let us look at the direction of the flow of the electric current that is drawn from the positive pole to the negative pole in electric circuit diagrams since Michael Faraday's time, which is the opposite of reality, as every bright student knows today.

Individuals who are not familiar with programming find UML too difficult, and then they incorrectly interpret the entire object-oriented approach [10–12]. It is possible to pick an acceptable set of concepts out of UML for non-programmers; nevertheless, most professional books and training sessions are too often unnecessarily based on programmer experience. Comprehensibility and simplicity of UML is corrupted by the following facts:

1. UML models contain too many concepts. The concepts are at various levels of abstraction, and sometimes they semantically overlap (e.g., relations between use-cases); and even their concepts sometimes differ. The same model can therefore be interpreted differently by an analyst and a programmer (the typical example is associations between objects).
2. There are several ways in the UML diagrams to show certain details in models (e.g., qualifiers and link class objects or state diagrams that are a mix of Mealy and Moore automata). It is up to analysts, which option they choose.
3. Some concepts are insufficiently defined – such as events in state diagrams; one UML symbol covers several different concepts (e.g., in sequence diagram the data flow between objects blends with control flow).
4. Although UML is generally good from the graphics aspect, some analysts do not like for example the same symbol of a rectangle for instance and class (they are differentiated only by internal description) as well as the direction of the inheritance arrow that leads toward the parent object in spite of the fact that in the codes of programming languages (even in users interpretations) inheritance is represented by opposite direction – from the parent object toward the descendant.

2.3 UML Support of Object-Oriented Approach

Although UML has the ambition to be truly versatile and is also registered as a universal ISO standard [6], it is true that the largest field of application is object-oriented analysis and programming. UML supports many object-oriented concepts, and there is currently no other "more" object-oriented as well as standard modelling language. The success of UML in practical usage is based on many successful projects where the software has been developed in C++ or Java, i.e., languages that use object-oriented approach.

Practically speaking, UML is associated with object-oriented software creation for many users who do not even know that UML has an overlap with other areas of software engineering, such as relational database modelling.

3 MDA Approach

Model Driven Architecture (MDA) is an Object Management Group (OMG) specification [13] based on fixed standards of this group. The main idea behind MDA is to separate business and application systems from the technology platform. This idea is not new, the need to create a separate analytical and design model has existed for quite some time. What MDA brings are procedures and ways to transform these models. The primary objectives of this approach are to ensure portability, interoperability (interoperability) and reusability through a separate architecture [14].

The MDA approach advises a complex system to evolve as a gradual transformation of three large models:

1. Computer-Independent Model (CIM) - This model, also known as the domain model, focuses exclusively on the environment and general requirements of the system, and its detailed structure and specific computer solution are hidden or unspecified at this stage. This model reflects customer's business requirements and helps to accurately describe what is expected of the system. Therefore, they must be independent of technical processing and describe the system in a purely factual and logical way. It does not require to know any details of computer programming, but rather requires knowledge of the real target environment.
2. Platform Independent Model (PIM) - This model deals with the part of the complete system specification that does not change according to the particular type of computer platform chosen. In fact, PIM mediates a certain degree of independence of a particular solution to a given problem area to suit different platforms of a similar type. It describes the behaviour (algorithms) and structure of the application only within those limits that will ensure its portability between different technological solutions. Compared to the previous model, it is supplemented with information (algorithms, principles, rules, constraints...) that are essential for solving the problem area through information technology. The big advantage of the PIM model is its reusability and therefore it can serve as a starting point for various assignments when it is necessary, for example, to change another programming language, the need to reuse some legacy component or data, etc. It's like abstract programming in an ideal programming environment. At this stage of development, the so-called expansion of ideas is also taking place, as the target environment has not yet restricted us.
3. Platform-specific model (PSM) - The latest MDA model, which is already platform dependent, combines PIM with a specific technology solution. There is a so-called consolidation where the previous ideas must be realized in a specific target computer environment with all the shortcomings and limitations of the particular version and configuration of the technology used.

4   Three Different Types of Class Hierarchies in the Process of Software Development

Conceptual hierarchy of classes, hierarchy of data types, and hierarchy of inheritance do not necessarily mean the same thing regardless all three hierarchies are drawn in the same way in UML, as we can only see stereotypes to distinguish among them in detail. These hierarchies have a strong connection with MDA ideas and can be recognized as follows:

1. From the perspective of the user/analyst – the instances of lower-level classes then must be elements of the same domain that also includes the instances of the classes of the superior class. It means that a lower-level domain is a sub-set of a higher-level domain. This hierarchy is also called the *IS-A hierarchy* or also *taxonomy of classes*. In specific cases, it can differ from the hierarchy of types because it does not deal with the behaviour of the objects at the interface; rather it deals with the object instances as a whole including their internal data structure. Formally, we can define this hierarchy of a superclass A and subclass B as

$$A \prec B = extent(A) \supset extent(B). \tag{1}$$

   This hierarchy corresponds to the CIM phase of MDA.

2. From the perspective of *polymorphism*. This is a view of an application programmer who needs to know how to use the objects in the system but does not program them. The object in lower levels of hierarchy then must be capable of receiving the same messages and serve in the same or similar context, such as high-level objects. Therefore, this hierarchy is the *hierarchy of types*. Formally, we can define this hierarchy of a superclass A and subclass B as

$$A \prec B = interface(A) \supset interface(B). \tag{2}$$

   This hierarchy corresponds to the PIM phase of MDA.

3. From the designer's perspective – new object designer. This is a view of a system programmer who needs to create these objects. This hierarchy is a *hierarchy of inheritance* because inheritance is a typical tool for the development of new classes. Formally, we can define this hierarchy of a superclass A and subclass B as

$$A \prec B = methods(A) \supset methods(B). \tag{3}$$

   This hierarchy corresponds to the PSM phase of MDA.

   In simple problems it is obviously true that these three above-mentioned hierarchies are identical. In more complex problems, however, this is not true – e.g., in the design of system libraries that are often re-used when developing specific systems.

4.1   An Example - Library of Object Collections

A good example is the Fig. 1 showing *IS-A hierarchy*, *hierarchy of types* and *hierarchy of inheritance* of a part from a system library of the Smalltalk language concerning collections of objects. A similar library can be found in each object-oriented programming language, of course. There are the following classes:

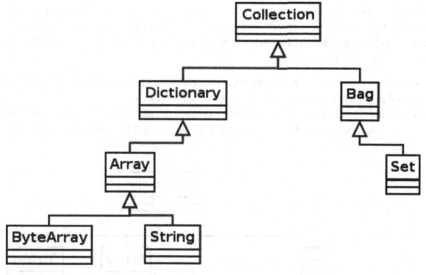

Fig. 1. IS-A hierarchy (*class taxonomy*)

- *Collection.* This is an abstract class from which the individual specific classes are derived. A common quality of all these objects is the ability to contain other objects as their own data elements.
- *Dictionary.* This is a collection where each object stored has some specific value assigned to it (therefore forming a pair), which serves as an access key to the specific value. Dictionaries can be really used for simple translations from one set of some values to another set of values. A frequently used example of the use of object dictionaries is a telephone book – the set telephone numbers is connected with another set of names of the people having these telephone numbers.
- *Array.* Simply said, an array is a special kind of a dictionary where the keys can only be integer numbers in the range of size of the set of values. So, the array values look also to be accessed as if through keys.
- *Byte Array.* It is an array where the permitted scope of values is limited to integer numbers in the interval from 0 to 255.
- *String.* A string of characters can be also viewed as an array where the permitted scope of values is limited to characters.
- *Bag.* This is a collection in which internal objects are stored inside without any accessing key.
- *Set.* This is a special kind of a bag where, as a restriction, the same value can occur only once. If the set already contains a specific value, another input of the same value is ignored unlike the above-mentioned bag, which allows multiple occurrences of the same element value, as it is corresponding with mathematical concept of sets.

This description of the classes from Fig. 1, however, follow the *IS-A hierarchy* (or *class taxonomy*) as we know it from natural sciences. However, we can define a slightly different perspective as it is presented at Fig. 2, but equally important as first one from Fig. 1. If we concentrate on *behaviour of objects*, we obtain a bit different hierarchy that is defined by the scope of permissible messages. We can also declare this different hierarchy as a *hierarchy of object interfaces*. It is the *hierarchy of types* corresponding with the PIM phase of MDA. This supertype-subtype hierarchy has following differences from previous *IS-A hierarchy*:

- Because *Dictionaries* can receive the same messages as *Sets*, they can be therefore viewed as subtypes of *Sets*. The same applies also for *Bags*.
- *Arrays* and *String* are interpreted as almost independent classes, because each of them supports their very specific *operations* (*messages*) with little common intersection.

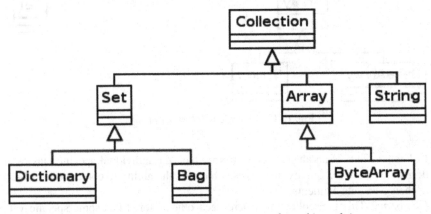

Fig. 2. Hierarchy of types (*supertype - subtype hierarchy*)

This second hierarchy is not yet the last one. We can create yet one hierarchy to match the PSM phase of MDA. See Fig. 3. This *hierarchy of inheritance* is very important for the programming when programmers have to code their objects in programming languages. Again, we will have some differences from previous hierarchies:

- *String* can be implemented as a special kind of *ByteArray* (e.g., inherited subclass), because separate character elements are typically encoded into bytes of tuples of bytes.
- Software code implementation of *Array* and *ByteArray* has nothing in common and therefore it makes no sense to inherit anything together. *Arrays* are implemented by pointers to the internal objects that make their elements, but *ByteArrays* are contiguous sections of computer memory where their elements are stored directly in particular bytes. Although these two classes have much in common and can receive the same messages in terms of external behaviour (that is, they have *polymorphism*), the code of their methods cannot be shared and it is necessary to program each method separately, although they behave very similar when receiving messages.

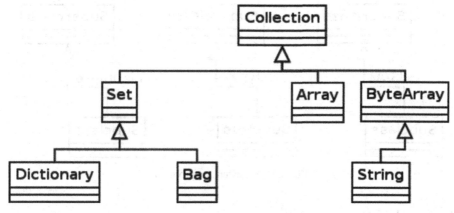

Fig. 3. Hierarchy of inheritance

5   Discussion - UML Support for Software Development Phases

In Sect. 4, we have just explained the need for different class hierarchies. The problem which remains to be resolved is how to express them in the UML class diagrams. Fortunately, the UML standard includes an extension mechanism that allows new concepts to be introduced in a standard way. They are so-called stereotypes. All we must do is select some graphic element, and we can give it a different interpretation by typing the text in double angle brackets «». The result is in Fig. 4.

Of course, if each UML class diagram clearly indicates what phase of the model it is (CIM, PIM, or PSM in the style of MDA, for example), then this additional stereotype is unnecessary.

5.1   The Need of MDA Way of Thinking

During system development it is necessary to gradually transform the system model into a condition that is necessary for physical implementation of the system in program code in the specific programming language.

According to our experience, initial objects cannot be viewed only as initial simplification of the same structure of future software objects, as the common error of the analysts in UML [15]. The initial business model can be simpler but – at the same time - it contains concepts that are not directly supported by current programming languages.

In the large project development, IS analysts face the problem when not all system requirements are known at the start of the project and the customer expects that discovery and refinement thereof will be part of the project. The problem is even more complicated because the function of these systems built has impact on the very organizational and management structure of a company or organization where the system is implemented – such as new or modified job positions, management changes, new positions, new departments, etc. Therefore, it is desirable to also address the change of these related structures during the development.

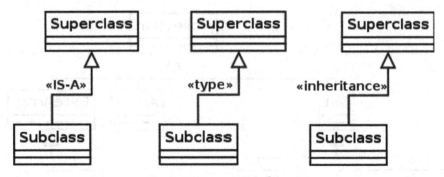

Fig. 4. UML extension proposal

6 Conclusion

In this paper, we demonstrated the need of a more precise interpretation of modelling concepts on an example of gradually transforming object class hierarchy especially in the conditions of agile development, where the documentation is very reduced, and misinterpretations could occur. Being agile cannot mean that we resign ourselves to precision and focus only on faster development at any cost. It would cost us in end-user satisfaction as well as future higher costs for maintenance and functional modifications.

Underestimation of the model differences in the individual phases of development of an information system results – in some instances of "real programmers" who think of themselves as agile developers – in such a simplification where analysis using UML is viewed as the only graphic representation of the future software code – typically in C++. Analytical models are then used not to specify the problem formulation with the potential users of the system who are also stressed by the complexity of the models that are presented to them. In our practical experience, many projects in UML suffer from this problem. In response to that, there are two "remedial" approaches used in practice: Agile Software Development [16] and Domain Specific Methodologies [15].

The objective of this article is not to suggest that UML is a bad tool. On the contrary, UML is a good and rich tool. The fact that it is not perfect in all areas is not anything horrible. UML is the first successful attempt to introduce a reasonable object-oriented standard, and it is good to use it. We only wanted to point out some of the problems that relate to the use of the UML. We see a danger that results in the fact that the UML is taught and used incorrectly. The problems discussed can be summarized as follows:

1. UML is not a method; it is "only" a standardised tool for recording ideas. UML needs some method, otherwise it doesn't help.
2. UML is complicated – people who are not familiar with programming have difficulty learning it. It is not easy to explain UML to laymen and non-programmers in just a few minutes at the first meeting.
3. Analysis in UML must not be a graphical representation of the future program code.
4. UML itself does not accurately emphasize which concepts are to be used in the analysis phase and which only in the design and implementation phase. Unfortunately, many books on UML look at modelling through the eyes of implementation and are

written in a language for programmers and particularly programmers in C++ or Java or a similar programming language.

The thoughts described in this article are a synthesis of our own experiences from project modelling at the international consulting company Deloitte, and Czech system integrator of telecommunications applications. Datalite Ltd, from own research activities and from teaching the development of information systems at the CULS and CTU universities.

References

1. Zemanek, H.: Al-Khorezmi his background, his personality his work and his influence. In: Ershov, A.P., Knuth, D.E. (eds.) Algorithms in Modern Mathematics and Computer Science. LNCS, vol. 122, pp. 1–81. Springer, Heidelberg (1981). https://doi.org/10.1007/3-540-11157-3_25

2. Knuth, D.E.: Algorithms in modern mathematics and computer science. In: Ershov, A.P., Knuth, D.E. (eds.) Algorithms in Modern Mathematics and Computer Science. LNCS, vol. 122, pp. 82–99. Springer, Heidelberg (1981). https://doi.org/10.1007/3-540-11157-3_26

3. Rumbaugh, J.: Object-Oriented Modeling and Design, vol. 199. Prentice-Hall International (1991)

4. Booch, G.: Object-Oriented Analysis and Design with Applications, 2nd edn. Benjamin Cummings, Redwood City (1993). ISBN 0-8053-5340-2

5. Jacobson, I., et al.: Object Oriented Software Engineering: A Use Case Driven Approach. Addison-Wesley (1992)

6. OMG Unified Modeling Language (OMG UML), Superstructure. Version 2.4.1. Object Management Group. Accessed 29 Mar 2020

7. Reed, R.: Notes on SDL-2000 for the new millennium. Comput. Netw. **35**, 709–720 (2001). https://doi.org/10.1016/S1389-1286(00)00204-8

8. John Hunt (2000). The Unified Process for Practitioners. Object-Oriented Design, UML and Java, p. 5. Springer, London (2000). ISBN 1-85233-275-1. https://doi.org/10.1007/978-1-4471-3639-2

9. Introduction To OMG's Unified Modeling Language™ (UML®). Object Management Group®, Inc. https://www.uml.org/what-is-uml.htm

10. Graham, I., Simons, A.J.H.: 30 Things that Go Wrong in Object Modeling with UML 1.3. University of Sheffield & IGA Ltd. http://www.iga.co.uk

11. Ambler, S.W.: Toward executable the UML. http://www.sdmagazine.com

12. Thomas, D.: UML – The Universal Modeling and Programming Language? September 2001. From the library at http://www.ltt.de

13. MDA® - The Architecture of Choice for a Changing World. Object Management Group®, Inc. https://www.omg.org/mda/

14. Noureen, A., Amjad, A., Azam, F.: Model driven architecture - issues, challenges and future directions. J. Softw. **11**, 924–933 (2016). https://doi.org/10.17706/jsw.11.9.924-933

15. Kelly, S., Tolvanen, J.-P.: Domain-Specific Modeling. Enabling Full Code Generation. Wiley (2008)

16. Beck, K., et al.: Manifesto for Agile Software Development (2001)

Author Index

E. Babkin et al. (Eds.): MOBA 2023, LNBIP 488, p. 119, 2023.
https://doi.org/10.1007/978-3-031-45010-5

Printed in the United States
by Baker & Taylor Publisher Services